The Worst Fishing Dog Ever

Ron Dungan

The Worst Fishing Dog *Ever*

And Other Essays

University of New Mexico Press | Albuquerque

© 2026 by Ron Dungan
All rights reserved. Published 2026
Printed in the United States of America

ISBN 978-0-8263-6920-8 (paper)
ISBN 978-0-8263-6921-5 (ePub)

Library of Congress Cataloging-in-Publication data is on file with the Library of Congress.

Founded in 1889, the University of New Mexico sits on the traditional homelands of the Pueblo of Sandia. The original peoples of New Mexico—Pueblo, Navajo, and Apache—since time immemorial have deep connections to the land and have made significant contributions to the broader community statewide. We honor the land itself and those who remain stewards of this land throughout the generations and also acknowledge our committed relationship to Indigenous peoples. We gratefully recognize our history.

Cover illustration: *Leaping Trout*, 1889, by Winslow Homer; courtesy of the Cleveland Museum of Art
Part openers courtesy of the New York Public Library
Designed by Felicia Cedillos
Composed in Chapparral Pro

To my late father, who took me fishing,

and my mother, who put up with both of us.

Contents

Part III. Dystopia

First Cast

I've got to get out of here. For four decades, I've lived in Phoenix, Arizona, a city built on the ashes of a tribal civilization known as the Hohokam, who built irrigation canals along the Salt River, planted crops in the Sonoran Desert, and survived for a millennium. It's hot here in the summer, and it has been painful to watch the city grow into a throbbing metropolis with bad air, crowded freeways, and pale night skies. But I have stayed because I've found work and made friends, because the winters are nice and the fishing is good.

Nobody sees that one coming. You picture Phoenix and think of saguaro cactus, palm trees and red sunsets, tile roofs, golf courses and suburban sprawl. Arizona has plenty of all that, but its landscape is complex, and layered—crawling with scorpions and diamondbacks down here in the prickly pear thickets and rising up to a mountainous labyrinth of chaparral, rising higher to woodland realms of juniper oak pine, where streams flow and trout rise, where smallmouth cruise the river bottoms, where days are cooler and stars shine bright. From time to time I tell myself I should leave, and make half-hearted passes through job listings or the high- country real estate market, but I'm still here: a fly-fisherman who lives in the desert, an anomaly, a contradiction, a work in progress.

I moved to Arizona in the '80s, a Midwestern transplant with few marketable skills and a passing interest in the outdoors, and worked various jobs to pay the bills: reporter, construction worker, printer, copy editor, page designer. By the time I circled back to reporter, I had a home in the suburbs, a pickup truck, a gun dog or two curled up by the fireplace, a bunch of fly rods in the closet.

For decades now I have roamed the West, looked out at blue horizons, navel-gazed at that place within myself that craved rivers and wild ground, a connection with the natural world that was palpable yet difficult to explain.

As it turns out, I am not the only one who felt this connection to nature that could not be dismissed with a wave of the hand, an eye roll: fun, hobby, playing out there. The late Edward O. Wilson thought this through and came up with a name for it—biophilia. Clever researchers have since made the case for biophilia by getting people outdoors to measure heart rates, blood pressure, brain activity, and other tangibles. They have concluded what so many of us know in our bones, that getting outside is good for you, and not just as a form of cheap therapy, but a vital part of what it means to be human.

And so I lived two lives, one that revolved around my day job with its endless stream of deadlines, emails, memos, and corporate initiatives. The other life I spent in the hills, where I measured the quality of my life by nights spent under the stars, mountains climbed, canyons walked, waters fished. At first I fished with bait, but then I learned to fly-fish. That's when things got serious, because fly-fishing opened up new worlds. I had a lot to learn.

Historians haven't quite worked out fly-fishing's origins. For years I heard that Dame Juliana Berners wrote the earliest account of fly-fishing. It turns out that others wrote about it before her, and all we know for sure is that the sport has vexed men and women for centuries. People describe fly-fishing in many ways: a way of life, a calling, a passion, an adventure, an art, a science, a challenge, an addiction, a culture, a cult, a way to experience nature, a waste of time. Ted Leeson writes that when fly-fishers try to explain their passion, they often wind up talking about rivers, birds, and trees—not so much the fish or the fishing but their surroundings. Biophilia research might explain why angling feels like such a balm for the soul. It's a sport for the gentle, the genteel, the curious, the artist, and the *artiste*, but it also rewards the resourceful, hard-working, blue-collar angler who puts in the time and effort. Fly-fishing is old trucks, leaky waders, duct tape; dumb luck, little white lies and real whoppers; rickety boats; favorite rods, bad roads, cheap hotels, mountain towns, burger joints and brew pubs, high-country camps in all kinds of weather; fishing dogs and old friends. We scan maps until our eyes bleed, talk to people, plan trips, bind luck and skill the best we can. We nap by the stream. We drive for hours to get to the water, caffeinated, white knuckled, music booming out of the speakers. We embrace the slow passage of time in a society obsessed with convenience. We work like the devil to catch a fish, only to let it go.

We let fish go in the hope that we might catch them another day, because as long as the sun rises and sets, we'll pencil fishing days on the calendar. Those of us who live in big cities, or Midwestern towns, or the Sonoran Desert, might have to work at it harder, but we'll be there, come April or May or June, where water runs cool and trout rise.

We might note that dams can disrupt rivers, but you can catch a lot of fish below the dam. The natives have gone—a sign of the times and a real shame—but wild browns have taken up residence. We adjust to various realities, form cults and clans based on our preferences for wild fish, or native fish, saltwater or bass or steelhead. Our little adventure awaits. Our home water calls. We'll dent skid plates and crack oil pans just to get to a fishing spot. We'll look back on days on the water, each one a gift, a body of work that embraces not just fish caught but experiences, memories stashed in the frontal cortex.

You thought it would be a hoot to do something different—move to the desert, buy a boat, take up rock climbing, backpack the Grand Canyon, learn to fly-fish. You stick around, put down a few roots, and the next thing you know life has barreled along and everything has changed. You could move somewhere else for a change of scene, or take up golf, but these things didn't seem such a good fit years ago, and they don't seem any better now. So you fish. You embrace slowness in a culture of convenience, sky above, river below. A silence settles in, not just the absence of sound but a presence, and time takes on new meaning. Your eyes on the fly, your thoughts on the slow speed of a stream and the shape of rivers, a trance broken by the quick strike of a brown trout. Wind comes and goes, the sun arcs and an osprey soars. You cast again and again, look at your watch and find that hours have passed. You didn't see that coming, but then again, you're not surprised.

Part I
Something Bigger than Ourselves

1. Old Trucks, Leaky Waders, Duct Tape

I NEED TO CLEAN up my act. My gear is a mess—vest smeared with floatant, rod handles worn, truck dirty. Stray ends of tippet dangle from my fly boxes. I live like a dirtbag, sleeping in the back of my truck, driving from one stream to the next. I don't cast, I dap, flop an Adams into some pocket water and on to the next spot, stick and run, my line loose, fly rod caught a willow thicket, feet sliding on rock snot and mud.

Maybe I'm overthinking things, but maybe I'm not, because somewhere along the line, fly-fishing got highjacked by poets, artists, and writers, and the simple act of catching dinner, of bloodsport, got tangled in narratives of soft light, tight loops, and dimpled rings on the water. In tradition, ethics, and philosophy. Certainly our best days *do* have a certain aura about them: days so idyllic you feel you have stepped into a painting. I'm not sure that elevates fishing to an art, but apparently anything can be art—even angling. Izaak Walton put it in writing, and we've talked about artful casts, beautiful flies, and handmade bamboo rods ever since.

Some of my memories don't line up with anybody's concept of art, however. I have fished late. The last truck flips on headlights and pulls out of the parking lot. I set my rod out of harm's way and crack a beer. The autumn chill comes hard and fast, my hands cold from releasing the last rainbow, my feet stiff. What a day. The wading boots come off and I drop them on the asphalt with a thunk. Off with the waders. I pull off a sock, feel the weight of it in my hand, and watch the drip, drip, drip on the pavement before I wring it out and toss it into the camper shell. The next sock comes off, not as bad as the first, but still a wet mess.

I put up with this for at least a couple of seasons, long after the waders had outlived their useful life. But waders cost good money, so I patched them and patched them, each time telling myself 'that oughta do it,' and still wound up with a pile of soggy laundry in the back of my camper shell.

The truck had about 300,000 miles on it but was in pretty good shape, even after rattling around gravel roads for well over a decade. Most trips were pretty routine, but the truck took some abuse. The night I drove home from a high-country lake in a driving rain, for example. We didn't catch many fish. My friend Eddie fell asleep in his float tube, drifted away, and finned back by late afternoon. We humped the tubes up the hill, and then the rain started about the time we pulled away. About nightfall. I remember fishtailing through the mud and hitting bottom a time or two. I lived out of that truck for days on end, fishing, walking, getting from one place to the next. It got me to the water, which made it a fishing truck, something that rarely makes it into that painting.

Our mental images of fly-fishing as art can take a beating when fish don't bite, when we slip on mossy river bottoms, when we fish with lead, but we soldier on. We stand under glaring sun or in freezing water for hours, lob teeny tiny flies we can barely see, can barely tie on with our cold fingers. Oh, how we suffer for our art.

Some days things really do feel as if the stars have aligned. Yet real life inserts itself into even the best fishing trips. We go back to camp and take a nap. The fishing slows down, so we go for a hike just to check out the scenery. I recently had such a trip. I made graceful casts with small delicate flies. I fished mayfly patterns and caught rainbows, browns, brookies, cuts. I followed rivers and tributaries, took hikes to alpine lakes. The green aspens of late summer, warm days, thunderstorms gathering high above the peaks and swirling about. The river, no more than a headwater creek at that elevation, ran low. Some fish spooked and fled. Others rose from cut banks. Asters blooming in damp grass. Birdsong.

Days passed and from time to time the artful pursuit of trout receded to the grim reality of life on the trail. I fished until my hands chapped and bled. Campfire embers snapped and burned my coat, which smelled like smoke and backcountry funk. Thousands of trees stood dead on the mountain, ravaged by drought and beetles. Cows bawled in the distance. They walked through my camp one morning, stomping and lumbering about, about half a dozen right outside the tent, crowded around the fire ring, dozens more passing by. My fly rod, leaning on a bush, could have been knocked over and trampled had I not gone out to chase cattle. Cow shit everywhere, the smell of it lingering. Put *that* in your book of trout poetry.

A few nights later I rose from a deep sleep on a high meadow to piss on the tundra, the air crisp, the sky clear. The Perseids fell from the heavens and vanished into distant peaks. The creek dried up in a long drought; the few remaining cutthroats darting in shallow lies. My broken heart. The drought followed me to the next river, to brown trout with the midsummer blues.

Yes, you *can* find a sense of poetry out there on the water, scenery so beautiful it makes your eyeballs hurt, a dance between man and nature that takes place when all goes well in the universe. But the universe can be unstable. Dark holes and crashing asteroids and dying stars out there, solar flares, gravity, and the earth's wobble. Drought and wildfire and rivers filled with mud and ash, so moments of Zen only make up part of the story.

Summer to autumn. The aspens aflame. The *Baetis* calling from a high desert tailwater, geese passing under a bright moon, the old waders replaced with new, the truck a newer version of the old. Slippery footing on that thing they call rock snot. Bobber fishing. A coiled leader, the pig's tail of a bad knot. Dry flies and mangled casts. A twenty-two inch rainbow doubled up in the net. The water aboil with rising fish. Duct tape on my coat, duct tape slapped on a Therm-a-Rest patch for good measure.

Is fly-fishing really an art? Paul Schullery, former executive director of the American Museum of Fly Fishing and author of several fishing books, writes that our noble obsession is craft, not art.

> Craft is generally defined as the creation of something whose primary function is utilitarian rather than aesthetic. Craft can involve great creativity and originality, even genius. So can art, engineering, and cooking. A fishing rod is, first, a tool for catching fish. A fly is, first, a tool for catching fish. A cast is, first, a process employed to catch fish. Some of these activities may be practiced so finely as to reach a high level of craftsmanship; some may even be practiced by genuine artisans. But they are crafts.

That doesn't really change much. We can admire a nice fly or rod, a graceful cast. The average American builds life around comfort and convenience, and fly-fishing reminds us that few things worth having come easy. If we practice, if we keep learning, if we put up with at least a little discomfort, we may be allowed to step into that painting, however briefly.

"Fly-fishing is this great adventure we have in a thousand little episodes," Schullery writes. "Fly-fishing is our chance to embrace the unmanufactured, to earn something honestly, and to give ourselves over entirely and passionately to a pursuit that is in some mystifying way both irrelevant and important. Fly-fishing drives us nuts and keeps us sane."

I think Schullery has a point, although definitions of art and craft can vary so that the distinction between them can get fuzzy. That does not diminish the various skills we associate with fly-fishing. They can take years to master. Yet this mastery is not crucial to catching fish, which began as a way to get dinner. A good mend can be more important than an artful cast. Some of us tie ugly flies, or average flies, and still catch fish. And sometimes we get lucky.

To most people, fishing seems like an escape from real life. Fish long enough and hard enough and lines blur, as if real life comes down to fishing and what most people call real life amounts to a nuisance. It happens. Some people fish enough that the grownups in their life start to worry. Their bosses complain, their wives leave. But living a traditional middle-class life can be overrated, in part because it is filled with baggage, in part because real life can be messy and unfair. A neighbor dies of a heart attack two months before—or after—retirement. A coworker falls to a cancer that comes out of nowhere. Knees weaken, vision fades, arthritis flares up in the cold, a thousand little wounds of time, until you've grown too old to wade a stream.

Fly-fishing teaches us that life is fleeting. A cottonwood leaf falls into a stream and floats away, another autumn around the corner. A generation of mayflies passes in a matter of hours. Every day brings new choices. We can chase dollars or search for something bigger than ourselves: writing, mountain climbing, painting, ultra running, hiking the Pacific Coast Trail, music, poetry. Somehow, in ways that are difficult to explain, fly-fishing seems to qualify.

All those late afternoons; the dimpled water, the caddis aflutter, maples turning, the trout in their autumn colors. We move lightly in that dance between man and nature, try not to step on nature's toes. Most of us have jobs, spouses and kids, dogs and mortgages, *responsibilities* that keep us off the water. But we get out when we can, while we can. It's a life.

A delicate strand of tippet snaps and a trout fins away. There's your poem. The one that got away, and the one after that. Duct tape and leaky waders and dog slobber and beat-up trucks, the sweet, musty scent of forest duff, aspens shedding their leaves, wet socks, woodsmoke, hook-jawed brown trout, burgers and fries, a tattooed barkeep at day's end, the jukebox blasting, embers that hurl themselves onto your jacket. Bugs. Bugs everywhere. Bugs on the water. Midges on your waders, midges clustered around your lantern at night.

Maybe we *can* call fly-fishing an art. Not casting, not tying, not building rods, but learning to live in the sweet spot of life, to dance on the world's trout streams. I think this is what Walton was getting at. We can't all make a living as guides or master fly-tyers or rod builders, but we can master a few steps. We go to our jobs, pay the bills, tend the home fires, raise families and still find time to fish, to chase trout or bass or tarpon on big water, where we learn that yes we can, by God, dance, step into the painting, sing our song, write poetry.

The loop is tight and graceful; the mend, the fly, tied well enough to catch fish, the rise, the life-and-death struggle, the release. Is it utilitarian if we let our fish go? Another rise, another cast, another day, until the sun goes down, the moon comes up, and we walk stiffly back to the parking lot. The dance ends and the stage lights dim. Off comes a boot. Off come the waders. Off comes the wet sock, the wringing and tossing into the back of an old camper shell. Geese under the rising moon, the night chill. What a day.

2. Clutter

FOR SOME OF US, taking up fly-fishing feels like falling into a black hole. On one end of the hole you see a young angler, a beginner without any gear. On the other end, someone with a dozen rods, a couple of boats, a room full of fly-tying material, and divorce papers on the kitchen table.

How do we get there? By fishing—first for trout, then bass: streams, lakes, maybe saltwater, getting by with what we have until, inevitably, a new destination means a new piece of gear. We buy waders and boots, a stouter rod. Reels and spools, fleece, floatant. A vest, float tube, and fins. Books and videos. Flies, flies, flies.

Fly-fishing can become another form of consumerism if you let your guard down. You start out with nothing, so you buy things. Some of them last, some wear out, and some get lost. Flies break off, reels get stripped, waders leak, tippet snaps. At some point, you have acquired an arsenal, backed by a fleet of small boats, a four-wheel drive truck. Backups to your backups. You wonder if you've overdone it.

You can avoid malls, tell yourself you'd rather have a root canal than shop, steer clear of Amazon, but stepping into a fly shop seems different. Go ahead, shop around, you're among friends here. The industry keeps developing new products—thousand-dollar graphite rods, boats, and expensive toys of all shapes and sizes, and you're tempted to add more to your inventory. But good gear can last a lifetime, and you eventually reach a point when you go into a shop and walk out with nothing but a few leaders and a spool of tippet. What you really need is more time to fish.

Fly-fishing helps you lose the clutter of everyday life. For some people that's the whole point. And while it won't solve your problems, it will help put things in perspective. The rat race fades into the background, and the toxins in your bloodstream drop to a reasonable level. Some causes of stress are the byproducts of growing up—work, family obligations, and so on. Others are hobgoblins of modern society, the never-ending stream of useless information and shiny things: television, social media, and cell phone noise.

At first the cell phone seemed like a good invention: a portable phone so you didn't miss a call or could dial up help in an emergency. But I could not help but notice that the first people who had them were salesmen with three numbers who never answered the phone. Before long, phones morphed into surrogate brains that could summon information quickly but lacked common sense, and here we are, connected yet distracted, addicted, zombielike, a cyborg nation. You'd think with all the digital innovations out there people would have more free time, but they have less.

Journalists and academics have found that technocrats have hijacked chunks of our lives, as they burn and pillage society on their way to the bank. Johann Hari writes that these grifters have stolen our collective attention span. Franklin Foer says they have stolen our privacy and our ability to think straight. Our health, mental and physical, suffers from various forms of digital bondage.

Conventional wisdom says the technology has arrived for good and there's no going back. But conventional wisdom can miss the mark. Things change, people change, and although we can't go back in time, we could make different choices. We could put down our phones, give the ol' frontal cortex a break. We could clear some space on the calendar, pack up and go fishing, drive into the woods with a sideways glance at our phones until we see the words "No Service," pull over, and make camp. That'll show the bastards.

Every road trip begins with a well-stocked arsenal of food and ice, a sleeping bag, and other supplies. It only takes a day or two, with all that stuff, before clothes and gear scatter hither and yon in the back of the truck. Flashlights, socks, pots, and pans burrow just beyond reach, until the camper shell looks as if someone threw a stick of dynamite into it, or raccoons have made themselves at home. About the time the mental clutter fades, this physical clutter takes over. But when I rearrange it, a new mess takes its place within half a day. The truth is you really need most of it. Maybe 10 percent is overkill—but which 10 percent?

The bucket list can turn into another form of clutter, if you're not careful. At first, it spurs us on to great adventures, but sometimes it gets in the way or leads to high expectations, which can weigh like an anchor. You want to explore new water, but a trip with too many destinations can become a series of appointments, another checklist like the one back home, only with better scenery and a campfire at night.

We fly-fish because we enjoy it. We find comfort in a day on the water. Enjoyment becomes obsession. Obsession becomes frustration when we show up at the water and learn that the fish want something smaller than what we have in our boxes, or something bigger. Something green. Something gray, something black. Because some days fish want nymphs, some days streamers, emergers, or dries. You get by wet wading in a pair of old shoes until November's chill blows out of the north, cold like daggers, and when you get home, you dig under the couch cushions for some loose change and hope you have enough to buy a pair of waders. You get by with a 5-weight rod until the day you try to throw a bass bug with it, or with a cheap reel until it falls apart. You get by.

The lost flies, the fish that reject our feeble offerings, the snapped line, it all triggers a reaction, and a promise: Never again. Never again will I fish poorly because I lack the proper gear.

So you stock up, armed with credit cards, tax refunds, and

whatever discretionary income you can muster. Fly-shop guy wants to help. Your wife has questions. Catalogues have pages of possible solutions to our problems and to problems we've yet to consider. The internet offers more choices, with websites, links, menus, everything you need with a few clicks, as they say, a shopping cart in the upper right-hand corner of your screen. You throw money at your failure to catch a trout, all the while knowing that fish don't care what kind of gear you have. But one day you realize you've gone too far: You have too much stuff. Not just a few backups, not just a little redundancy, but a real mess.

You try to cull some gear from a pile in the garage that would fill a small U-Haul. You could swear that some of it got dragged in during the Nixon administration. The yard has grown feral—knee-high grass, leaves and fallen branches, weeds, a rusted wheelbarrow, the neighbor's chickens, shovels, and rakes. A family of badgers has burrowed in by the back gate. The house needs paint, the dog gnaws on the carcass of a small mammal, and your wife howls that you have a whole closet full of dubbing and tinsel. You'll get it all done—hacking, hauling, digging, mowing, trimming, weeding and edging, shoveling and hammering, sorting and tossing. You'll make a few trips to the Goodwill, work your to-do list like a pro. You'll manage, you really will.

You go back inside because you remember a trip you keep meaning to get on the books. You grab your calendar, pick up the phone, shoot off an e-mail. Then you decide your gear cull can wait. You dig through your stuff, quickly, purposefully, because in spite of the volume you know where to find everything you need—rod, reel, waders, boots, vest—in a matter of minutes. You load the truck, gas up, and go.

When you get to the stream, fish start to feed, just out of reach, and you've got to work out a casting angle, or a mend. No, time on the water won't solve your problems, but it's a good start. Sunlight and storm clouds chase one another on the horizon. Trees sway and a black hawk soars, caddis flutter, and the water sings. Your mind wanders, and for half a second you find yourself looking back at that young angler without any gear, as if that black hole has opened, for just a moment. Then a fish rises, the hole closes, and you cast.

3. Hard Work, Dumb Luck, Little White Lies

SOME ANGLERS WOULD RATHER be lucky than good. I know I would. These are the words of Lefty Gomez, who understood that luck and skill can be intertwined, but also had a sense of humor. Gomez, a pitcher for the New York Yankees, made this crack about baseball, but the words have lived on and, through the internet's magic, morphed into a serious question, as if one could choose to be lucky. A lot of Americans don't understand luck or chance. You see this at the blackjack table, the stock market, the trout stream.

Fly-fishing takes skill, but luck has a funny way of inserting itself into a fishing trip, as it does in life, both good luck and bad, in doses large and small. With luck, you will get to the water safely. With luck, the gods will smile on you, the wind won't blow too hard, the hatches will come off, fish will bite.

Frequently, what fly-fishers think of as luck actually amounts to timing. These things are not identical but can amount to the same thing. You try to time hatches, weather, stream flow, and some combination of these things, but a lot of times you're guessing, and it's a good idea not to overthink it. The best fishing trips blend luck, skill, and good advice in such a way that you feel both good and lucky.

"One of the things you eventually learn as a fly fisherman is how to accept luck and generosity as if you deserved both," John Gierach writes in *No Shortage of Good Days*.

A lot of people who preach about the virtues of hard work have amnesia when it comes to the various strokes of luck that went their way: economic tailwinds, windfalls, and serendipity. Lots of people work like the devil and barely get by; others find success but don't lose perspective—such as Gomez, the quick-witted lefty who grew up on a homestead where he woke up at 4 a.m. to milk the cows and muck the stalls.

Gomez made his famous crack about luck after his outfielders ran down and caught three fly balls one inning. He also once attributed his success to "clean living and a fast outfield." He may have been talking about the same game when he said that; the record is unclear.

The idea that fishing requires luck probably comes from a more traditional form of angling—sitting on the bank with a worm on a hook. For the most part the angler chucks the bait out as far as possible and waits. When a fish bites, it *feels* like luck. If it happens several times, it begins to look like skill. No doubt, bait fishers make decisions that improve their odds of catching a fish. He chose the right spot, tossed his worm over a drop-off or a weed bed where fish might come in to feed. She made the cast, concealed the hook, and so on, but bait fishers must wait for a fish to come their way to eat.

Fly-fishers don't take as much for granted. We learn basic casts and mends and move on to the bow and arrow cast, flipping, and roll casting, so we can target fish that hold in hard-to-reach places. We stalk and crouch, watch and wait. We buy floatant to keep our flies buoyant, weighted line to make them sink, tippet to make our line all but invisible. We learn how to read a lake or stream and key in on places where fish feed, tie up special flies: these for trout, those for bass, these for emergers, adults, larva. Mayflies and midges, ants and stoneflies, caddis and sculpins. We sight fish, keep an eye out for risers.

Along the way we pick up boats—kick boats, row boats, belly boats, drift boats, rafts, and canoes—to get our fly out to the fish. Just chucking it out there and waiting won't do. We invest time and money in our craft, never doubting that we must hone our skills and have the right gear. We make calculations and educated guesses, all the time knowing that a little luck never hurts.

But sometimes, like our angling brothers and sisters who sit on the bank throwing out worms, we just cast and hope for the best.

Picture a small lake in the pines. Maybe you have fished it a time or two, but you don't know much about it, and you aren't catching anything. It rains, flying ants hit the water and trout begin to rise. You dig through your boxes for black dry flies—about anything that floats will do. You cast, skillfully and mindfully, near some risers you saw a moment ago, and start catching fish. Sure, you paid attention and tied on the right fly, but the rain, the ant fall, the rising fish, all amount to timing—or luck.

Some anglers will make up for bad luck with lies, which come in all shapes and sizes. A vague fishing report that leaves a lot to interpretation: We caught fish, or, we did all right, for example. Nothing wrong with that. Less humble anglers will drag in numbers, score cards, spreadsheets. Numbers can jog our recollection, perhaps elevate the story to legend—the fish taped out at twenty-eight inches. They can also create the possibility that the story is bullshit: fifty fish. A hundred. Twenty-eight inches, pounds, feet.

Our obsession with numbers is a sign of the times, a nervous tic in today's fast-moving world, in which everything breaks down to income, profit, share price, and net worth. So some people naturally transfer that thinking to the trout stream—numbers of fish caught, size of fish, nothing but the best gear money can buy—the usual trappings of a consumer society that doesn't know when to quit. Focus too much on keeping score and then a trout, speckled and free, becomes "number seven," to paraphrase Thomas McGuane.

Fishermen lie. You take that into account when talking to other anglers, even guides. Anglers can also lie to themselves, most of them little white lies, the standard internal dialogue and chatter that loops through the brain on a fishing trip: This stream fished better in the old days. I'll organize these fly boxes when I get home. Twenty inches. One last cast.

Somewhere along the line lying about fishing became an industry and a way of life—magic rulers that turn an eight-inch fish into a real whopper, hats and T-shirts that proclaim all fishermen lie, a wink and a nod at the bar when a known bullshitter gets going.

"What happens to the chronic smeller of flowers, watcher of birds, listener to distant thunder? Certainly, he has lost efficiency as an angler," McGuane writes. "Has he become less of an angler? Perhaps. This is why fishermen are such liars. They are ashamed of their lollygagging and wastage of time. It's an understandable weakness. In some of today's brawny fish camps, flowers and birds can raise eyebrows."

Ethical standards must be maintained on the water, whether you smell the flowers or fish until your fingers bleed. Pack out your trash, keep a few fish, if you must, but release the rest, and try to leave the place the way you found it. More and more, that might mean keeping your mouth shut.

This is why anglers are such liars when they talk about *where* they fish. They're vague. They mumble. They make stuff up. Because not everyone shares our love of rivers, or trout, not to mention silence and solitude.

Some consider this vagueness unnecessary, selfish, or elitist. In my experience, those who insist that everything is up for grabs don't spend their weekends bouncing on back roads looking for new spots or uncrowded ones. They tend to have easy access to information the average angler might have to dig around for or jobs that allow them to go fishing on a Wednesday. And they remain silent about the hordes of weekend warriors who trash campsites, take home more than a limit, and set the forest afire. They say nothing about people who leave cans and bottles, tents, sleeping bags, dirty diapers, tampons, toilet paper flapping in the breeze, nothing about fire rings full of melted glass and charred aluminum, rotting food, Styrofoam, and plastic. Yes, we should share fishing spots willingly, but cautiously, with the appropriate filters in place. There's only one world, which we must share with poachers, hooligans, and litterbugs, the urban masses and their mantra of Me, Me, Me.

And so we lie. We lie to protect rivers. We lie to protect the fish and our fellow anglers, to honor promises made to friends. We stay mute on social media, vague in conversation, stone-faced and bald-faced, because sometimes a little white lie is not enough, and we turn to the nuclear option, tell a real whopper—the fishing is horrible, the fishing is so-so, the fish are all small, there are no fish in that stream that I know of.

We can work hard, hone our skills, wear that lucky hat, ban bananas, but there is no substitute for being there. By showing up at the right time, you improve your luck. Fish. Fish more, as often as possible. Something might happen. The only guarantee is that you won't catch fish sitting at home. Call it luck or skill, timing or hard work, or some combination of these, but you set things in motion when you step out the door.

Fog on the water, the press of current, a fish at the end of the swing, the dumb-luck trout that keeps your interest when things slow down. You're a good angler—capable and self-reliant. You've read the water, gotten a few takes, and played a good fish as if you've done it before. As luck would have it, you have another day of fishing ahead. You're not superstitious—not one bit—but you'll probably wear the same hat tomorrow.

4. Sloth

IS IT JUST ME or has fishing become a lot like work? I see a lot of overachievers out there these days, people who offer up all kinds of advice on how to catch a trout: You have to put in your time, fish a size twenty-eight, row across the lake, walk five miles in a driving rain. It's rise and shine at 4 a.m., or you're wasting your time, pilgrim. Do you want to catch fish or not? What's *wrong* with you? For a time I bought into this. Sometimes I still do.

But I like to think there's a place for the lazy and unfocused, the slothful angler who naps by the stream. Let us not forget the slug who shows up long past daybreak with a belly full of breakfast, a head full of daydreams. Here's to the dawdler who stops to take a picture, smell a flower, watch a heron rise above treetops, to the camp layabout who intends to fish just as soon as she finishes this chapter, to the guy who has never fished international waters, though he'll allow that the brochure looks nice. Let's raise our glasses to lollygaggers and slackers, the angler who bypasses crowded tailwaters to fish small streams at a leisurely pace.

I don't mind working for my fish. That's guide speak for keeping a line in the water and maybe changing flies or spots frequently. A guide who says this wants to manage expectations. Nothing wrong with that. The day starts out with a fish or two and slows down, another fish or two and then nothing, and so on, until you look back at a decent day. And I don't mind getting up early once in a while, though it's not my preference. In my youth I worked construction and woke before the sun came up. Then I spent a few decades working the late shift, which put my internal clock in a blender and dropped it into a time zone somewhere in the Pacific Ocean. My schedule might pass for normal these days, but I sometimes work into the night when all the early risers, the lazy bastards, start to get ready for bed. So while I generally don't fish early if left to my own devices, sometimes it's part of the deal. When a guide says 5 a.m., you show up.

Some water really does fish better at first light, but sometimes this is just Puritan bullshit. On high-country lakes, for example, an early start buys you a few hours before the wind picks up and blows you off the water. And fish do bite then. But on some rivers the hatches don't start until 10 a.m. or noon. The slothful angler quickly learns to tell the difference, which gives rise to the notion that he has paid attention, plans his day carefully, and gets a good night's sleep. It makes you wonder whether he's lazy or smart.

Sometimes you have to get on the water before anyone else because other anglers will show up and spook the fish by 10 a.m., which makes you wonder whether you should just look for a less crowded stream.

But we live in frantic times, and I sense that money changers and overcaffeinated types who want to prove something have hijacked our simple pastime. The Serious Angler shows up in all the fishing magazines, both print and digital. No place for the slothful on these pages, which are all business, the covers splashed with big steelhead, big browns, big 'bows, held by square-jawed men or fetching young women with pearly teeth, holding the fish of a lifetime with a wry smile that suggests they do this every day. You see blurbs for stories on the best places to fish, the best anglers, the best gear; promos for stories about tactics, strategies, and secrets; a quiver of adjectives for the size of a fish: big, huge, giant, monster, heavyweight, gator. The images imply that if you buy the magazine, you, too, might catch a monster brown, but you have to put in the work. Christ, I need a nap just reading about it.

The same has happened with the hiking crowd, which once celebrated the writings of Henry David Thoreau and Ed Abbey, the solace of the great outdoors. Some have written off Thoreau and Abbey as hypocrites, either because they haven't read them or because they take them too seriously. They overlook the fact that although they were philosophers, they were also humorists. Many popular ideas about Thoreau don't hold up to scrutiny. Yes, I find him a bit thick, but I can also manage a few passages from time to time. He can be both thoughtful and amusing, and those who assume he was a recluse get it wrong: "I think that I love society as much as most," he writes. "I am naturally no hermit, but might possibly sit out the sturdiest frequenter of the bar-room, if my business called me thither." Those are not the words of a misanthrope. In any case, loafers and barstool philosophers have fallen out of fashion. A ninja warrior clan has taken to our trails, elite athletes who never quit, who set out not to experience nature but to conquer it. They keep meticulous records and have infused hiking with cash, marketing concepts, and technology. They walk hundreds of miles in a matter of days—and on purpose. They don't walk up the mountain, they run. A lot of anglers have followed suit.

Everyone looks so *serious* these days. The smell of money is in the air and it won't go away. I think that's because our society has crossbred fishing with a jock mentality. The results are predictable: weekend warriors with cell phones in hand, who don't want a quiet day on the stream to catch a few fish. They want an Instagram moment. They want action, a body count, something for the cameras. They want mama gator. Can we get some video?

The slothful angler knows that most trout streams are quiet places, packed with fish that will never make a magazine cover. He'll be all-business when the fish start to bite. She might snap a few photos if she lands a good fish, but she also embraces the time between those moments to take in Thoreau's broad margins in life, or McGuane's longest silence. You can have a good day on a trout stream just by showing up, and you don't have to get there early, or fish until dark, or use secret flies, or special tactics, or strategies, just a dead drift: not a tactic but a basic skill.

I've seen articles that talk about influencers and sponsors, a raging debate about who gets featured on those magazine covers and who gets free stuff. The modern media landscape rewards expertise in Search Engine Optimization and social media, a never-ending cycle of self-promotion, more than it rewards actual expertise. We can thank marketers and Silicon Valley for this, the grifters who have inserted themselves into nearly all aspects of our culture, so it should come as no surprise that this might extend to fishing.

Some say people have changed because of the internet and social media. That's the money talking. The digital world may have fried a few brain cells and shortened our collective attention span, but it hasn't fundamentally changed human nature. I believe the digital world has amplified some of our worst tendencies. It has removed filters and tapped into our phobias and insecurities, our social quirks, our proclivities for gossip and mob violence, our dark hearts, our greed, our apathy, our lust. It has made us prone to distracted driving.

An arrogance drips off of the prose of this new breed, but that's nothing new either. It existed in 1895 when George M. Kelson wrote *The Salmon Fly*. Kelson, who had no Instagram, no Twitter handle, no cellphone, was "dismissive of amateurs," and "smirked at the 'uninitiated,' the 'novice,' and those 'so low down in the scale of ignorance' that he couldn't tell a Jock Scott fly from a Durham Ranger," Kirk Wallace Johnson writes in *The Feather Thief*. "Of course, neither could a salmon, but in order to justify paying for such costly feathers, some needed to believe that the fish could distinguish between the twenty shades of green described in the masterworks of fly-tying."

As I said, social media haven't really changed us all that much. They amplify. They shine a spotlight on the human condition. They blather on.

Even the amateurs seem a little jacked up. There's a competition on the water, a walk and a talk that has seeped into fly shops, as if the magazines have done their work and produced a class of Super Anglers. These people fish hard, by God, as if their lives depended on it. They talk of hundred fish days and twenty-two-inch fish as though these things happen all the time. They could have been guides themselves, if only their lives had gone differently. The slothful angler flips on his bullshit meter and finds the needle in the red.

You can still find lakes and streams out there without cell service, the quiet places of the world where life moves without schedules, without calendars, other than winter, summer, spring, fall, sunup and sundown, and the bright afternoon in between. A breeze stirs, a hatch comes, fish rise, or don't, and your biggest decisions are fly changes and how far to walk. The closest you'll come to a work mindset is walking a little extra, or putting off lunch, because the fish start to bite. Come to think of it, you forget lunch altogether, but a thermos of coffee and a few snacks await in the truck.

So I salute you, slothful angler, the one who works the ten-to-noon shift before taking a long break, then considers her options. It's good work if you can get it. It's called fishing, what some people do on their days off. Here's to anglers' hours, sleeping in and puttering around camp. Here's to the half-assed, the sleepy, the laggard. Here's to the retiree who has actually retired. Here's to the absent-minded, the guy who shows up late, leaves early, and doesn't care who knows it.

5. Stealth

BROWN TROUT CAN BE moody bastards. One day they are predators, grabbing bugs, flies, mice, and toddlers with savage takes; the next they sulk on the stream bottom. So I didn't bring a lot of optimism to the water, a small stream in Arizona. Early November, the creek low, the trees bare, the trout spooky.

Low flows and months of tourists thrashing the water had turned these fish into prissy Chicken Littles, but I did my best and fooled a couple. The casting windows were small, tight openings in willow and bramble, or narrow lanes in cut banks—some difficult, some routine. After a couple of hours I came across a nice pool under a low-lying bush, bare of leaves, but still a fly-grabber. The trick was to flip the fly upstream and drift it under the branches. I nailed the cast and got a strike.

It was a good fish, and I got him away from the branches, into open water, where he flipped off the barbless Adams. Sure, I wanted to land him, but I still had my fly and didn't stress the fish, so I walked away feeling pretty good about things: the cast, the drift, even my stealth, because the fish held right in front of me.

A few years back I spooked a lot of fish on that stream, and it occurred to me that I had spent a lot of time fishing places that don't require much stealth. I wondered if it had made me lazy. I wondered if I shouldn't step up my game, try harder, get on my hands and knees, do some *work*.

But hooking that fish got me thinking about a lot of different kinds of stealth—various techniques and tackle choices that we make so often we don't give them a second thought—thin tippet, small dry flies, dapping, crouching, moving in shadow.

In *Fly Fishing Small Streams*, Gierach devotes a whole chapter to stealth called "Sneaking Around on Your Hands and Knees." It was a relief to reread it.

"I do not spend the whole day sneaking around on my hands and knees and probably wouldn't enjoy it too much if I did," he writes. Instead, he talks about sidearm casts and keeping a low profile when you approach a stream. You crawl in for a good fish from time to time, but "each situation is unique." He recalls a friend who "duck-walked" to a pool, then went "on all fours—all threes, actually, with one hand holding the seven-foot rod out behind him—until he could kneel behind one of those squat, Oriental-looking trees." He got the fish, but ruined the pool. So it goes.

One kind of stealth we bring to the game involves how we approach the stream—slowly, a bit hunched, using bushes and rocks for cover. It helps to drop to a knee, to stoop or hunker down, and it's usually a good idea to stay out of the water, which is contrary to human nature, because current against your legs feels good.

"Current is a mysterious thing." McGuane writes. "It is the motion of the river leaving us, and it is as curious and thrilling a thing as a distant train at night. . . . Things that pass us, go somewhere else, and don't come back seem to communicate directly with the soul. That the fisherman plies his craft on the surface of such an element possibly accounts for his contemplative nature."

Current can consume your thoughts if you let it; the way it passes like time itself; the way the surface of the water marks a line between two worlds. Ideas that probably aren't original but seem relevant, significant, perhaps important, crowd your thoughts. The real reasons to get into the water are not philosophical, or spiritual, but practical. You get in to cross the stream, to move into position for a better drift or to get your shadow off the water. Other than that, it's best to avoid splashing around.

Tippet choice amounts to a form of stealth in fly presentation, but it involves a tradeoff. Fish a light line and you get more hook-ups, but you also break off more fish. If the trout don't get a lot of pressure, you'd be surprised how readily they take flies attached to something stouter, such as 4X, and you can land them quicker.

Landing fish quickly can also fly in the face of conventional wisdom, which says that you need to play a big fish on a stout rod and let him run. Sure, let him go for a bit, if for no other reason than to see what you're up against and maybe take the edge off, but after a few decades you get a sense of what the right amount of pressure feels like. One reason to land the fish quickly is that it won't stress the fish as much. The other comes down to simple math. Shit happens. The longer you play the fish, the greater the odds that something will go wrong.

The downstream cast also flies in the face of conventional wisdom, which says that you fish dry flies upstream, and, in general, you do for a number of reasons. For one thing, fish look upstream. Also, the old timers did it that way—it's traditional, something in the old books, something codified on certain English streams, an ethical choice on others. Nothing wrong with that. On crowded waters, you can also run into references to high holing, low holing, fisticuffs. But these traditions go back before catch-and-release waters created trout with PhDs in flies and tippet size, a sixth sense that allows them to tell your imitation from the real thing. Assuming you have a stretch of water to yourself and you're not on an English chalk stream, sometimes you can fool these fish with a downstream cast, followed by a few rod shakes to get a drift, so the fish sees the fly first.

I have a few seven-foot rods for small-stream fishing, but most of the time they stay in the closet. I have found that though you may not get tangled up in the willows casting a seven-foot rod, a nine-foot rod allows you to move in closer, flip the fly into the water, and dap to the fish. That solves not only the casting problem but also the mending problem.

In *Fishing Bamboo*, Gierach writes that some people get a short rod because they're spooking fish. "If you're spooking fish with an 8-foot, 5-weight rod, the answer probably isn't a 7-foot, 3-weight. The answer is a longer leader and a better cast."

Americans are a noisy, raucous bunch. Fly-fishing goes against the grain of popular culture for a variety of reasons, and its quiet, contemplative nature is one of them. ATVs roar by in a cloud of dust, campsites fill, generators drone, cows bawl, gas pumps thrum on hilltops. You pass ghosts of old machines that once rattled and boomed day and night, fallen silent as they go back to ground; the concrete and rust, bricks and beams, and rotting fence posts. You drift flies over riffles and pools and listen to the stream, try to imagine the clamor the mines made more than a century ago. Perhaps a few miners wet a line when their shifts ended, catching a few for dinner as their fellow muckers and blasters worked downstream.

Fly-fishing frequently takes us to places that may or may not carry a wilderness designation but have wilderness qualities, such as silence and solitude, which can also go against the grain. You have to scan maps and put in hours of research to find these places sometimes, but even then, you never know what's out there until you walk.

Picture a lake in southern Colorado. It sits at around twelve thousand feet above sea level, and it's full of brook trout. I've fished it twice and never seen another angler. A few years ago I took a pack raft there and fished until thunderheads reared up and chased me off the water—dark clouds that tossed lightning bolts over the peaks and bellowed messages from God: time to go; get off the mountain; Jesus is coming.

The lake feeds a river with about half a dozen tributaries, each with its own personality. One stream has eager young fish, another has a series of meadows that break up the fishing as you go upslope, including a slow section with big surly browns that dash for cover as you walk along the bank. After a few days of nothing but marmot chatter and thunder, you begin to appreciate not only the peace and quiet that a trout stream can offer but also the variety of experiences possible in a week of fishing. You learn to adjust your stealthiness to the situation at hand.

And so I have moved into new territory, using stronger tippet, a longer rod, small dry flies. I move quickly, release my fish, tell lies when I get back home. Another kind of stealth: moving through country in a way that leaves the water the way you found it—litter free, with strong, healthy trout that aren't too freaked out. It means speaking softly when you talk about your favorite spots, treading lightly, keeping your fires small, and packing out your trash.

The year had passed in all kinds of fishing where stealth didn't matter much: river smallmouth, eager brook trout, tailwater fish that don't spook easily. I showed up at that skinny Arizona stream feeling a bit rusty, but after I hooked that one good fish I didn't beat myself up as much.

I have seen anglers lay out long casts on this water, one of them with a fourteen- or fifteen-foot leader. It's possible I have made a few long ones myself. The quiet pools between stretches of fast water harbor some suspicious trout—just setting foot in them, gently, some fifty or sixty feet away, can put risers down. You create a small ripple when you do that, and even the best cast will do the same. At some point, you have to accept that certain fish present a challenge. You make the cast, but something's not right. The fish lie low. The drift, which you thought looked pretty straightforward, happens slowly and takes your fly off course, just out of the feeding lane, which could be why the fish hang in that spot in the first place. You have choices when this happens—change flies, wait to see whether the fish rises again, or move on to the next pool. Maybe I should summon up my patience with these fish, settle in, wait them out, but I usually don't.

Patience can amount to another tool in your toolbox, a form of stealth, so long as you stay out of the sight cone and the fish keeps feeding. You can overthink this because, as Tom Rosenbauer points out, fish don't always behave the way books say they do. They move sideways, change direction, and swim downstream. Every piece of water is different, and a lot of variables play into what trout see and how they react.

"You are going to get it wrong, and you will spook fish. It's part of the game, so don't agonize over it. Move on to the next one," he writes.

It felt good to get on that water and fool a few brown trout, the moody bastards, but I had a sense that things had started to wind down. I went back about a week later, the sun out, a stiff wind out of the hills, not many bugs. The stream had that autumn aura, a sense of loss and a feeling that someone had stacked the odds against me. I may have gotten a couple of looks, but no takes. Time to move on, go home or try some new water. I took the dog for a walk and stopped by a put-and-take lake to get in a few more casts before heading home.

I strung up a 6-weight rod and threw buggers and nymphs into the lake, where a few fish rose in the shallows. I stripped, paused, counted long and short, retrieved fast and slow, changed flies often. There wasn't anything stealthy about it, but the weather was nice, the lake quiet. The buggers and nymphs didn't work, so I tied on an oversized Griffith's gnat, otherwise known as a dead chicken, on stout tippet. Nothing stealthy about that either, but I landed a couple of nice rainbows that I brought in quickly and turned loose. I felt pretty good about my choices that day, and made a note to come back to the lake the first chance I got. Sometimes it feels good to just stand there and cast without all that sneaking around.

6. It Beats Working

THEY SAY DON'T QUIT your day job. It's an old joke about aspiring poets, musicians, artists, writers, and generally good advice. But day jobs can be overrated—good for the wallet yet bad for your health, because work has become, for many of us, a sedentary grind. Yes, plenty of people out in the big world swing hammers and fit pipes, lay brick and build things for a living. But much of the workforce has changed in my lifetime. A nation of farm and factory workers has become a nation of office grunts, with legions of the aspiring: desk jockeys, middle managers, balding salesmen, software wranglers, and marketing gurus. They stare at computers, catch planes, sit through meetings, and catch up on paperwork back at the hotel.

He pounds the computer keys, lays low, and rides corporate tailwinds. He is soft in the middle. She butts her head against the glass ceiling. Weekends pass catching up on emails and planning, the weekdays packed with phone calls, software updates, meetings, meetings, meetings. For days on end, they make their way through a climate-controlled digital overlay of the real world, the world of whimpering beasts, blood in the water, thornscrub, tooth and bone.

Fly-fishing allows us to drop in on what's left of the real world, if only for a while. You feel the rough edges of a trout's lip, the soft grass, cold that knifes under your jacket. The two worlds pull at us, but the manufactured world frequently prevails because "you gotta eat," as they say, and most of us need money to do that. So we soldier on at the computer, one day at a time, hope for the day when we can fish more and work less, which does not come.

I haven't swung a hammer for a living in decades. In those days, you could find work on a construction site just by asking, and if you showed up every day, you would survive the first round of layoffs. Working outside had some advantages, even on days when the mercury pushed 105 degrees. Less stress. Good exercise.

I needed those jobs to pay the bills between newspaper gigs because writing can look more like a meandering road to the poorhouse than a career. You might as well say you want to fish for a living. But over time I managed to carve out a career as a common laborer in the cubicle farm. Sure, it had plenty of downside, but so did construction. I came to like my desk jobs. And so I've sat on my ass for a living ever since.

Choose a job you love, the old adage goes, and you'll never have to work again. I've had several jobs I loved, and, yes, it does beat working, but so does fishing. I stepped away from the daily grind the first chance I got.

Few of us fish every day and most of us probably wouldn't even if we could. McGuane was right—even in the world of bums, lip-rippers, and addicts, fishing remains a respite from work for most people. For a lot of us, that means sitting and gazing at a screen, until the eyes burn and the back aches.

Why do we stick with these jobs? For the money. I doubt the fly-fishing world as we know it would exist without the desk jockey. Who else can walk into a shop, lay down a piece of plastic without a second thought, and walk out with a thousand-dollar rod? But a lot of middling desk jobs don't exactly pay big bucks. The price tag of most big-ticket items in a fly shop can make an average working stiff laugh, cry, or wince. Those prices lead some people to call fly-fishing elitist, though that's not the word that comes to mind when you see a guy on the river who lives out of his truck and eats cold beans for dinner. Sure, you can find lots of ways to throw money at the sport: private water, new gear, international travel, fancy lodges, but all those shiny toys don't really define what we do.

"At its core, fly fishing is about simplicity," Kirk Deeter writes. "It's a stick and a string. It's basic. And despite all the jargon, all the sales pitches about space-age graphite in fancy rods . . . fly fishing is primal." Deeter started fishing as a kid, pitching spoons, riding to the water on his bike. He made the tackle switch when he got older. It's not the gear that fascinates him, he says, it's the mental challenge, the puzzle, figuring out how the pieces fit together.

"That's a brain trigger that appeals to a certain type of personality," he writes. Sure, some lucky anglers have enough money to take up the sport without thinking too much about the cost of gear. The rest of us have to figure things out and make them work, which can challenge the household budget and wear on the frayed edges of a bad marriage. We put off fixing the truck, or the leaky roof, so we have money to fish. Gierach sums it up nicely: "A friend once asked, How come a guy who dresses in rags and drives a smoky old pickup can afford such snazzy tackle? It should be obvious."

For every angler who can spring for the good stuff right out of the box, you'll find several who get by with used reels and patched waders. They build their own rods. They tie flies. They learn how to stretch a dollar and bring a resourcefulness to their craft that keeps them on the water in spite of economic challenges. For every angler in an overpriced hotel, you'll likely find another boondocking on Forest Service ground.

They wake in the cold to rain on the tent, snow on the windshield, their wading boots frozen blocks of ice. The extended forecast looks grim, but they can stick it out another day or two. They figure it out as they go. They thaw out with a cup of coffee, grab a couple of fresh leaders at the shop, and head to the water about the time the clouds break, and then they cast. There. Big fish in the seam. That one. Again.

Fly-fishing draws people from a variety of backgrounds, incomes, and experiences—gentlemen anglers, CEOs, rogues, dirtbags, men and women obsessed with trout in a society obsessed with money, which has permeated every aspect of our lives: our politics, our religion, our education, music, art, sports. When economics rears its ugly head at a fly shop, we sometimes flinch, but more often just shrug. Ya gotta eat, and that goes for tackle manufacturers and retailers.

Occasionally I glance at reports on fly-fishing demographics, but it's more fun to people-watch at the Texas Hole parking lot at the San Juan River, the famous New Mexico tailwater. This backs up what the market research says: The sport skews to white folks in high-income tax brackets, but you'll see all kinds. The college kid in a beat-up Subaru, a few graybeards with wading staffs who take their time, the middle-aged stick with an accomplished demeanor who rigs up with a quiet efficiency, men and women of various ages, pay grades and ethnicities who ditch work, drive like banshees, pull on waders, fiddle around with fly boxes. Most look as if they know what they're doing, or they're at least off to a good start. They shake the calendar for extra days off and find time to fish. They make time. This is the new breed, the trout jockey, the person who might live in the suburbs but does not keep up with the Joneses, who devotes a spare bedroom to fly-tying, fills the garage with kick boats and belly boats, the closets with gear. They tolerate the day job because it pays the bills but keep work at arm's length. Promotions go to someone else in the department, who does not fish.

I don't think I've ever heard a cross word spoken between anglers at Texas Hole, though I did once hear a guy talking on a cell phone while he rigged up, trying to help some folks locate something on the computer. His frustration mounted, and I got the sense they wanted him to come into the office. He said, "Look, I'm trying to fish, and you're blowing my shit up."

We come to the water to get away from the office, the job site, the factory, the sound and the fury of everyday life. We're not sure why we do it, exactly, and I don't think a lot of us think about it all that much. It's fun. It beats working. We joke about this a lot: The best time to fish is when you can, or a bad day fishing is better than a good day at the office.

Nobody gets to fish for a living. Not guides, who untangle knots, change flies, and tell you to set the damn hook for a living; not the guy who minds the fly shop; not the salesman who peddles tackle. Not the video producer, the photographer, the scribe, who get paid to produce what the corporate wingnuts call "content" these days. They may spend more time on the water than the average person or might get to play hooky once in a while, but they do not get paid to fish. As far as I can tell, the only people who do are the folks on commercial trawlers.

While the workplace has changed over the years, fishing, and the fish, have stayed pretty much the same. The size of your bank account doesn't matter to a trout. Some days, the pieces of the puzzle lie scattered on the table, the fish in a mopey funk, the prospects grim, and everyone on the water has a rough day. Other days the rods bend and the nets come out. Eventually, we start to miss clean sheets and hot showers. We crave a cheeseburger and an order of fries.

We make peace with our work, fish when we can, leave when we must. On the drive home, we think we need to do this again soon. Real soon. Maybe we already have a trip on the books, or the part of our brain that plans stuff has gone into overdrive. Either way, we'll be back.

7. Little Man

The Worst Fishing Dog Ever

LET'S GET THIS OUT of the way: The dog doesn't die at the end of the story. He's here by my side as I bang away at the computer. He spends a lot of time there lately, his best days behind him, but he's still with us, a tail-wagging German Shorthaired Pointer. His name is Luke, but he has all these nicknames: Mister Luke. Mister Dawg. Tailwagger. Buddy. Snaggletooth. Little Man. Crazypants. He's the latest in a run of German shorthairs I have had over the years, and he's a bad fishing dog.

I got him as a long-eared pup with sound breeding and lots of promise as a sporting dog, the versatile kind that will point upland birds, fetch waterfowl, and track game, so he took to the water right away. The breeder lived in western Arizona. I picked him up on a hot summer day and drove out of the desert with the air conditioner cranked up until I got into the high country near Flagstaff, where we made camp down the road from a small lake.

Morning came, cool and cloudy, the fishing slow until a brief shower triggered an ant fall and I landed a few. When the fish stopped biting, I let the dogs out of their kennels and walked back to the lake. Sage went fishing, or what passed for fishing in her world—cruising the shallows to chase minnows, but Luke stuck with me. I walked into the lake, knee-deep without looking back, and puppy followed. He paddled around, and I watched him a bit, then left the water. The lesson took: Luke loved to swim. After a while he wouldn't just wade into the pond and go for a few laps—he launched himself like a torpedo, his body airborne until his chest hit the water with a sploosh, the sound a fat guy makes when he does a cannonball in the pool.

The usual puppy memories roll by: puppy teeth, puppy yips, puppy games, puppy dreams. He's in the backyard, chasing birds, lizards, or bugs. He goes through various growth spurts that make him resemble other animals—potbellied pig, giraffe, otter, wolf.

One day we load up the truck and go backpacking on a little mountain stream. By the time we drop packs, we have enough time for a few exploratory casts. The rods bend, the fly lines move, the pup gives chase, because casting and throwing look about the same to a dog. He's in a long-legged, high-energy phase, and wants to splash in the water and retrieve what we throw. I tell him no, no, no, trying to be firm, but it's hard not to laugh. Perhaps it is not funny. Puppy, says Jason, is the worst fishing dog ever.

But it all worked out because the next day came on bright and cloudless, the fish took our flies, and by day's end pup sat on the bank and watched. I thought he had learned, that we had an understanding, but I was wrong. He was pretty much a pain in the ass every time a fly rod came out, and I learned to separate the dog and fishing whenever possible.

German shorthairs have two gears—high and higher. They shoot out of the truck like bottle rockets, sparks flying, a puff of smoke, and they're gone. Put more than one on the ground and it's like hunting in a beehive. Every dog is different, but in general they have good noses, bird sense, drive and stamina, a touch of grace when they go on point. A good breeder will add an off switch, but there are no guarantees. Luke had an off switch.

Watching a pup grow into a sporting dog can feel like this little miracle in your life. One day you've got a goofy furball who eats bugs and chews on his foot; the next you watch a grown-ass dog sprint across the bird field. He slams on point, doesn't move a muscle. Now mister bug-eater is all business.

By the time he fills out, puppy weighs seventy pounds. Luke turned out to be an excellent hunting dog, but I never did quite finish him. In retrospect, if I could go back, I would have changed a few things that happened in some early training sessions. I also would have trained less and fished more in the summers, hunted more in the winters, and let things take their course. But it's too late for that.

He's up there in years now. We had a lot of good days, hunting and fishing and rambling around. When I say fishing, I mean he would ride along, and I would let him out of the truck for a spin while I rigged up or took a break. He was a good camp dog. And a lot of times he stayed with my girlfriend while I fished.

One advantage of training so much was that I could get Luke to heel or whoa on the water. It took me years to figure it out, but he lost his mind the most when we went smallmouth fishing—all those long casts, the woolly bugger sailing through the air and dropping into the water with a plop. In his mind, it was a game of fetch, with no actual fetching, and it drove him crazy.

One day I took him along when I fished for Gila trout, flipping dry flies with short roll casts. I barely heard a peep from him until I caught a fish. He'd whine a bit, get close to the action, maybe try to bite the fish, but for the most part he just watched.

A couple of wet winters rolled by and I heard talk of some banner quail seasons, but life got in the way. We had this minor health issue one season. Me—not the dog. A heat wave followed the next season on opening month, then a pandemic, a new job. I had things to do, but I figured we'd get in the field when the weather cooled down and the season got into full swing. In the meantime, we went fishing—brown trout in Colorado. Smallmouth in eastern Arizona. I couldn't help but notice he'd lost a step.

His range has narrowed and one day he flat-out quits, lies down to take a breather and does not get up for a long time. He's out of shape, I tell myself. He had a long hot summer of lying around. Not long after this the vet tells me Luke has an enlarged heart. Oh, he can fetch a duck, maybe a quail or two if we don't have to walk too far to find them, but for all practical purposes, we're done. His hunting days are over. I guess that makes him a fishing dog.

He's ready to fetch a stick at camp, a toy in the living room. He has pills to take, twice a day, but life is good. He's a goofball. He likes biscuits. He prefers my girlfriend's truck to mine. He's particular, and meticulous, and so we come up with a word for this: "particulous." He's at my side. He's a good dog.

It's possible to break down life to the dogs we keep. They remain part of our story, long after they have gone. There's Homer, the pound dog, a real mess, not unlike me when I got him, drifting from job to job and trying to get my feet under me. There's Nicki, a dog I found in the want ads, back when they had want ads. Here's Gambel, my first puppy. A real bird dog, and quite the runner. I settle down. I get married, take up fly-fishing. Along comes Blue, not long after the divorce. I spend a lot of time in the hills. When Sage comes it's not clear where I'm going in life, but I have steady work, something that resembles a career. I also drive around with three dog boxes in the back of the truck, a traveling circus of high tails and floppy ears, runaways and face-lickers and campfire buddies. Life goes by until there's just Sage, and so I get Luke, and now there's just him. I'm sure there's some rough sailing ahead, but I promised you that Luke would be with us in the end, so let's leave it that. God, he's a good dog. He's goofy and particulous, the worst fishing dog ever. But he's all right. I think I'll keep him.

8. Trout Chowder

SOME PEOPLE THINK IT odd that a person would go to all that trouble—gear, gas, drive time—just to catch a fish and let it go, but most people don't give a lot of thought to how the fish got there in the first place. The easy answer, that God put them there, or they evolved from some ancestral salmonoid doesn't hold up in these days of man-made lakes, stocking programs, urban masses, easy access to water, and industrial tourism. Overfishing, dams, agriculture, ranches, industry, roads, and logging have taken a toll on native trout, so biologists stock a lot of our waters.

We can't personally tear down dams, clean up the water, or adjust irrigation schedules, but we can turn a trout loose. People release their catch to leave fish in the river for tomorrow, or next week, or next year.

But the discussion of whether to let your fish go or not can grow heated. One discussion pits bait-fishers against elitist fly-fishers, who exchange mild insults—such as snooty fly-fishermen, or worm soakers. It's a myth that all fly-fishers are wealthy, but most of them can afford dinner. So can most bait-fishers.

Fly-fishers like to catch fish with rods they have built and flies they tie with their own hands; others want to eat fish they catch with a well-placed cast from a well-positioned boat. These sentiments are not identical, but they're similar. Fly-fishers revere Izaak Walton and reflect on the art of catching fish with an angle and all that, but forget that Walton ate his trout.

Another discussion pits animal rights advocates against those anglers who abuse the poor fish not for food, but for *sport*. Schullery addresses this at length in the title chapter of his book *If Fish Could Scream*.

> It is . . . both glib and penetrating to point out that proponents of catching fish only if you're going to kill them are in the odd position of seeming to prefer the death of the fish, while the catch-and-release angler they vilify prefers the fish to live. Who, we might ask, cares more about the fish?
>
> Here the glib and the penetrating intertwine almost inseparably. No doubt the fish, in the net or hand of a given angler, would vote to be released. But no doubt the fish would also vote not to have been caught in the first place, and that is the point made by the critics.

At the time, studies showed fish "lack the necessary biological equipment to feel pain or experience awareness as humans understand those terms," Schullery writes. This might seem obvious to anyone who has held a fish and looked at its mouth, which is hard and toothy, more like cartilage or bone than flesh. Nature has given fish a tool with which to grab things in a world full of sharp objects—crawdads, crunchy bugs, spiny fish, bees. One would presume, by looking at a trout's toothy maw (and thinking about it), that a hooked fish does not feel pain the way a human would. They may feel panic, but seem to get over it. Those who imagine otherwise are anthropomorphizing. They also fail to note that the fish might eat us if the tables were turned. We now have studies that show the fish does feel *something*, though we can't tell what. Is it pain? Yes. No. Maybe.

Some of us *do* think about the fish, not by anthropomorphizing, but by attempting to "connect with the fish's struggle for survival on much more profound levels," Schullery writes, tuned into the "moral complications of the moment." We have considered all the options, and decided the fish should live.

This does not raise us to higher moral ground. The reason we let our fish go is not an ethical one. The world has grown crowded, the planet home to billions of people, fed by industry, and if everyone kept their fish, there wouldn't be any.

Most Americans don't think about this because they have severed all connections to the food chain. Big agriculture, feedlots, fish farms, factories, and genetically modified organisms help fill supermarket shelves where suburbanites grab boxes or packages wrapped in Styrofoam and plastic, race home, and fire up the stove so they can eat before their favorite TV show comes on. This industrial grub—cheap, convenient, and well packaged—separates us from the nitty-gritty of getting our own food. We have abandoned hunting, gathering, and growing what we eat and cut ties to the natural world, a trade-off that affects body, mind, and spirit. Nature is beautiful, serene, its prose purple. Nature is a food chain, a messy buffet of flesh and bone, blood red, the music a chorus of howling screaming braying. Most suburbanites remain confused about nature, in part because they experience it through television, screen savers, and only occasionally by hiking and sightseeing. They anguish over the killing of animals, but give little thought to the death of rivers, vanishing dark skies, plowed habitat, mass extinction, or the collapse of ecosystems. Something is wrong.

Animal rights and animal liberation advocates who condemn fishing fail to see the "world as it really is," Malachy Tallack remarks. "Both are profoundly anthropocentric, and both seek to brush aside the complexities of biology, to impose straight lines where none can be drawn." They don't draw from a love for the natural world but a "deep revulsion at that world, and their prescription—that we should withdraw further from nature—only emphasizes this biophobia." They're not always wrong—feed lots, factory farming, and sloppy hunters present ethical problems, but hominids have eaten meat for more than a couple million years.

Our obsession with food likely began when one of the ancestors laid a mammoth rib over the coals. In *Death Comes for the Archbishop*, Bishop Latour considers a bowl of soup: "When one thinks of it, a soup like this is not the work of one man. It is the result of a constantly refined tradition. There are nearly a thousand years of history in this soup."

After a day on the water, you feel good talking about fishing over steaming plates of food. Toss the bones aside, open a bottle of wine, a beer the color of honey, throw a log on the fire while moths circle furiously around the lantern, the table strewn with dirty dishes, the empties in a small pile. As though Viking lords have dined. You sit back and reflect on the day with a sense that you've earned this meal, the knowledge that there are plenty of fish in the river, and tomorrow's another day.

A few years ago, I ran across a recipe for trout chowder in a short story by Ron Carlson. I caught and released hundreds of trout before I got around to trying it. I'm not against keeping a fish to eat now and then, in principle, but catch and release becomes a way of life. The big fish that live in quality water are powerful incentives, and old habits die hard.

One year I kept a couple of trout, and we gave the chowder a try. We got to the store, made a lot of substitutions with the ingredients, but wound up with a good meal. I haven't kept a trout since. They belong in lake or stream, native or stocker, while I remain a visitor, a tourist, with a cooler full of food and an itch to get outdoors. I do keep a few smallmouth occasionally. I dip them in flour, egg, and crushed saltines and then fry them up until they turn golden brown. But for the most part I release my fish and try, as Schullery says, to remain tuned to the complexities of the moment.

I smile when I recall Gierach's line about how a trout bum would rather go hungry than eat a trout. I skim a few lines of Walton and wonder what he would think about today's state of angling with its bag limits, slot limits, catch-and-release waters.

Fishing began as a way to get a meal, but our pastime was born when someone went fishing even though the tribe did not need food, Roderick Haig-Brown observes. We can imagine this through the mists of time: he steps away while everyone naps, she leaves a pile of wash by the river and tries her luck. Perhaps later, with mead, someone tells a story by the fire, with much laughter and grand gestures, arms spread wide.

9. The Backcountry

EVERY CAMP FELT SPECIAL, though they all looked about the same. Flat dusty benches, clusters of oak, a fire ring on a lonesome river bend. Paradise. That blank spot on the map, where dirt roads snaked through juniper and ponderosa to the canyon rim. We would park, shoulder packs, and walk down to the river of dreams. The internet did not exist. The fish would bite like crazy.

Some of my best fishing trips have been in the backcountry. Years ago, I assumed if I walked far enough and spent a night or two, I would catch more fish and bigger fish, but it didn't always work out that way, and so over time I learned to temper my expectations. Fishing the backcountry bundles fishing and walking into a hybrid experience, though one or the other can easily take over the narrative. There are a lot of different ways to fish the backcountry. Some people cover a lot of ground, others just want to get a little way from the road. Sometimes you do find good fishing out there. The quiet, solitude, and dark skies are a bonus.

The academic and mainstream press have churned out thousands of pages of purple prose and sober discourse on wilderness, so much stuff that you might think we would have a handle on the subject, but we don't. The late Sherry Simpson wrote that the term "wilderness" reminded her of "basic gun safety, be careful where you point it and always assume it's loaded." Fly-fishers have avoided the messy debate over wilderness that torments academia and some corners of the public at large. They'll argue over dry flies versus nymphs, browns versus natives and other fine points, but whether you catch trout near a gravel pullout or seven miles from the parking lot is your business.

Backcountry anglers don't necessarily talk about wilderness, though they'll allow that the view is nice out there. Most anglers understand that you can't find ground that no man has ever seen. They have given up looking for virgin waters, which do not exist. They want an experience, something other than ordinary life, which for many of us has become urban, sterile, predictable. They want to see a few stars, soak in a little peace and quiet, lose the crowd, find a stream that hasn't been loved to death. That's getting harder, but it's possible, and one way to find it is to walk a mile or two. That's as true today as it was thirty-five years ago.

Most of us start out youthful and optimistic, walking more miles than other anglers so we can catch more fish, perhaps a few lunkers. But in some cases, the stream will get skinnier, the fish smaller—something you didn't consider when you looked at the map and came up with a harebrained scheme to outwalk the competition. Sometimes you need a good walk to clear the cobwebs and see what's over yonder mountain. Streams that looked good on paper turn out smaller than you pictured, trails fade with age and grow over as government trail keepers, bushwhackers, sawyers, and muleskinners turn their attention to other routes. Maps work themselves into your brainpan as trails connect and as lakes, those blue dots on paper, become real places—cold and lonesome—where the trout are willing and the flowers bloom.

Maps can help you navigate the backcountry, but they don't offer much in the way of fishing advice. You set off with Lunker Lake at the top of your list, but along the way you pass half a dozen lakes and a couple of small streams, places that fly shop dude didn't say much about. The history of some Western waters is well-documented, but a lot of remote high-country lakes seem to fall through the cracks. Some don't have names. Some have trout, some don't. Some have natives, others have been stocked by dropping fish from a small plane, a practice goes back decades. Biologists come and go, records get lost, natives lose ground to stockers, or hybrids, and lakes pass from institutional memory. You talk to people and get the sense that most don't offer much, but also that nobody really knows—you have to wet a line to find out. That means hitting the trail with a fishing buddy or two, or a solo hike.

The solo trip gets a bad rap in today's world of ubiquitous cell towers, guardrails, and safety nets. Some say it's dangerous to go into the backcountry alone, but you may be safer hiking solo than going with the wrong person. Some nights a fire and a good dog can be all the company you need, and we are never really alone out there. You walk alone, fish alone, eyes on your drift, yet the pulse of humanity beats within, a steady drumbeat in the soul. We are social animals who came up through wilderness—singing and chanting, fishing, the flames rising, coals warm and red. You have the benefit of that experience and everything that followed: generations of hunting and angling, marks ancestors have left on stone, centuries of craftsmanship in the fly rod, lies told in camp. Your DNA comes wrapped in a double helix of civilization and culture, bits of Gore-Tex and graphite.

These memories keep bubbling up to the surface, a lifetime of trips boiled down to a few details: fish landed, meals cooked over hot coals, a mountain storm, the company I keep.

For five days, I wander headwater streams in southern Colorado, working out of a base camp near the junction of three tributaries full of wild trout. I call them the Three Amigos. Drought had knocked the stream down considerably, but fish hung along cut banks and riffles and took small dry flies. They also took big green drake patterns, though it was August, long past the hatch. Some days I dawdled and fished close to camp, others I took long walks to distant lakes. The aspens aquiver, storm clouds dancing in the peaks, asters adding dots of color, and morning dew. Songbirds and forest duff, my feet sore, my breathing shallow, rainbows, browns, brookies and cutthroats, a skinny route over sparse tundra.

I follow game trails in the Arizona high country, trails with bear scat and deer tracks that fade into brushy tangles and dark thickets, reminding me that we share these places with others.

Rain pours. And pours and pours. We hunker down and the campfire sputters and dies. Days pass. The creek is up, the fish down, clouds swirling in the peaks. When the storm lets up, the creek clears quickly and a few fish come to hand. But my girlfriend has had enough. We pack our gear and head out. When I spot some risers in a pool, I wonder whether we should stay, but the forever rain returns, and I race down the mountain, a metal rod tube strapped to my back as lightning flashes out of the peaks.

I lie on my back in a meadow, eyes heavy with sleep, the Perseids raining fire in the sky, the stream close, the trout in their pools.

We go up the mountain, cross the runoff of late winter storms, the current knee-deep and fast. We totter across with heavy packs, summit, head back down. The fishing is poor.

This tromping around the wilderness, marching up saddles and peaks, boots scuffed, legs stiff, the soggy, tent-bound nights, dodging legions of fun hogs—it never gets old. I've packed fly rods on Grand Canyon backpacking trips, mountain climbing excursions in Colorado, and the New Mexico high country. I reach the bottom, or the top, fish a little along the way, and wonder later whether lugging the extra gear was worth it. The answer is yes. Hell yes.

Backcountry routines can range from military-style marches to lazy base camps within sight of a trout steam or lake, where rainy afternoons can be spent napping or reading. Mine have evolved. I suspect they have for all of us. I take my time now. One day I'll be too old to care about long marches or logging big miles, and one day I'll be too old to carry a pack.

All those miles of logjam and deadfall, thin air and steep trails come back as the night passes. Campfires can get a bad rap in this world of overused trails, trashed camps, and megafires, which can lead to fire bans, finger-wagging, and hand-wringing among tightly wound tree huggers. They're not always wrong, because some people get carried away, but fire has a tradition which, like fishing, goes back to ancient times, and can be managed with woodcraft and an ethos of leave no mess. Burn it down, put it out before you go, and pack out your trash. Tread lightly.

Decades have passed since I took up fishing the river of dreams. In photos, it looks ordinary. In the summer, it gets warm and dusty. Banks once clear have grown over in weeds, the camps abandoned, and piles of driftwood have washed downstream. Bears roam, crawdads dash for cover as you splash across the river, the water knee-deep and cool, the summer nights. The smallmouth in their holes—God, how the fish would bite. They are still there, even in these days of drought and megafire and dark times. Up along the headwaters, clusters of old spruce tower and sway. Their branches droop with folds of old man's beard, and native trout rise in pools where they have been since Pleistocene glaciers rearranged the ground.

The backcountry calls: a lonesome bend of river, stars aloft, moonlit cliffs, the cool, thin mountain air. Flames dance, our shadows grow long as we stare into the embers. It takes us back, the way fishing takes us back, to the primal and innate. Memories blur. Dusty benches and shady groves. Cool nights, rainy afternoons, the brookies and cuts, the snowy peaks. Howls come out of the night woods, then stop. A deep silence follows.

10. All the Fish We Cannot See

WE TRY TO EXPLAIN, but our words get tangled or swept away in the wind. We catch a moment on canvas or film, but it falls short. The perfect light and snowcapped peaks look stunning, the trout in bright colors, ready for the spawn, but a photo can miss details that define the moment: your beating heart, cold water, a stiff breeze, the feel of the bent rod in your hands. Fishing appeals to the sense of touch, and our attempts to describe it in visual terms fail. Film can't capture it. Video remains a poor substitute for the real thing.

We gaze into a river and see nothing, so we place our hopes on a wish and a prayer riding on mayfly wings. We know for a fact that trout live in this water or that, but we frequently fish blind. We wear dark glasses, polarized to cut the glare, watch for risers, learn to read lake and stream, which tell their stories in a Braille of water and stone, logjam and weed bed. We move through this world slowly, deliberately, like the blind protagonist in *All the Light We Cannot See*, Anthony Doerr's novel about two young people who grow up during the Second World War. Cast. Mend. Repeat.

Sight fishing is a hoot, but some fish are too deep, some waters too murky. Trout in fact often seek out places where you couldn't see a fish if your life depended on it. They go to these places when bugs don't hatch, when the sun rides high overhead, when people thrash the water with bad casting or too much wading. They go there because the world is a dangerous place, full of ospreys, herons, bigger fish, and that band of weekend warriors with graphite rods. Some offer shelter, a place to hunker down and wait out danger. Others are food delivery lanes, with bramble above, rocks and roots and braided seams, places where a trout might grab a bite to eat, unseen and unmolested.

Americans live in a visual culture, our days and nights spent staring at screens of all sizes. We embrace the visual so much that we break down angling success or failure to landing the fish to bring it into our world, if only for a moment, because we want to *see* it, hold it, lay it against the rod handle, pose for a photo, watch it fin away.

In *The Old Man and the Sea*, we do not see the fish for days. The old man knows that he has hooked a good fish, so he keeps steady pressure on it, and the fish begins to pull the boat. It haunts the old man's thoughts as the boat moves into deep water, and it's a good fish and it keeps moving, farther and deeper. Days pass before he can turn it and move the boat back toward shore, the sun warm, the nights sleepless. At last he catches a glimpse of the marlin as a dark shadow that passes beneath the boat.

"He can't be that big," the old man thinks, and, pages later, "I want to see him, . . . to touch and to feel him." Numbers flash through his mind. The fish weighs more than fifteen hundred pounds, "maybe much more." He tries to calculate its worth, at thirty cents a pound, but gives up because he would need a pencil for this math.

Several times he thinks it is a shame a fish so grand must die, but it will feed many people, and he is, after all, a fisherman, and not some fancy boy catch-and-release fly-fisher but a real man, a Hemingway character with saltwater in his veins who can harpoon a shark in his sleep. It is ironic the old man's troubles begin when he can see the fish, touch the fish, claim the fish as his own, but he must.

That is the deal we make when we step into a boat or walk a

stream. As catch-and-release anglers, we let our fish go, but there's a chance the fish will tire and weaken, even die. Catch-and-release remains, on balance, a good practice, but Deeter writes that it carries a mortality rate and dozens of factors can play into that. Most fall along the lines of tackle selection, water temperature, hook barbs, fish handling, and how they intersect. Hook a fish on 7X tippet on a hot summer day, battle him for ten minutes, hold him aloft to snap a bunch of photos, and you might as well eat him.

We could stay home, but somehow that doesn't feel like the right choice. Like the old man, we must fish. Some call fishing an addiction, but there's little academic literature on this. Some bright young PhD candidate will probably figure it out some day. She'll do brain scans, hook up anglers to machines that map gray matter, and trace flashes of dopamine in the same brain cells that fire when we drink whiskey or make love.

Just getting outdoors can light up these dopamine centers, which explains why we enjoy every trip, even a fishless one. You walk to the stream, feel the wind, watch hoppers fling themselves across the grass, the sun's arc. It feels good out there, by God, walking to the water, not a care in the world. We send out prayers that float downriver. Hope rides on a breeze.

There. Cast there. Fish a dry and you can see the take. Strip a bugger and you can feel it. Fish a nymphing rig and the take looks wishy-washy, a limp handshake, a peck on the cheek. You're never sure about that bump until you set.

Nymphing rigs can also be a pain in the ass. Sure, you'll catch fish if you use one because fish spend most of their time feeding under water. I've heard eighty percent and I've heard ninety percent—it's difficult to verify either. This reduces fishing to a math problem, which leads to more math: two flies, six or seven inches to a foot apart, the split shot riding about eighteen inches or so up from that, et cetera. Watch the indicator carefully. Set on each twitch or pause. Fish with a guide and he'll get in position where he can see fish, but you might be blind. He'll watch your fly, the fish, the lips that barely move, the gills that flare and there! Set! You missed it. Clean your fly. Recast. I can see a dozen fish in the seam. Eighty percent.

When you hook one, you feel this life-force at the end of the line. You assess its size, the amount of line you have out, take note of root balls, boulders, and weeds, the hazards that could reduce your chances to land the fish. Your brain locks in, and you see color and light, hear the splash and smell the fish as it leaves the net, but the experience ultimately appeals to our sense of touch. The tug draws us to the sport, the struggle, the feel of line slipping through guides, the rod coming to life, your heart beating as a big boy makes his final run. You wet your hands, remove the hook, lift him gently, and release him. Blind again. You take a few steps and recast.

See the stream, cool and clear and running downslope, fast or slow depending on snowmelt or rainfall and geological tilt. Here and there the banks rise sharply or level off, the water flows and bugs hatch with the season and beasts howl and drool beneath the pale moon and we say their names: elk, raccoon, coyote.

We tend our home water, imagine a world not so grim, a world with plenty of room for dreamers and optimists, for those who believe in nature, ecosystems, willows, and trout.

But we live in dark times and the threats to our little pastime keep mounting: pollution, wildfire, climate change, overfishing, dams, roads, drought, housing developments, and no trespassing signs. Most Western streams eventually get harnessed by dams, diverted and fed through turbines, divided among farmers and golf courses and subdivisions, until a river, wild and free, home to trout and elk, becomes another math problem: cubic feet per second, acre feet, kilowatts per hour.

Fishing is a con game, the art of deception, each fish a mark, each cast a simple ruse. But we con ourselves as well with elaborate stories of getting back to nature when in reality the government diverts streams and manufactures lakes for a number of reasons, including our amusement. Ed Engle called it the paradox of tailwater fishing—dams can be hard on rivers but good for trout. We can reject various lies about rivers and fish and nature, but it seems like over-thinking things, most of them beyond our reach, and at the core of the fishing experience lies a truth: the world reduced to feelings, which are primal, simple, and likely traceable back to the Pleistocene. We must fish—we feel it in our bones. That passion lies at the heart of our world, and it's as real as anything else in American culture.

If we don't want to fish tailwaters, we can always look for wild fish deep in the high country, find a place with shaggy spruce trees, an old soul. You can still find such places—modest streams that run shallower than your average tailwater, with fewer or smaller fish, but they evoke the same feelings, the same blindness, same optimism. We catch fish in this seam but not that one. We fish a deep hole to no avail, only to catch a few in skinny pocket water around the bend. We push on, trust our feelings, spin yarns because we believe in rivers and creeks and trout.

Cast. Mend. Set.

It can't be that big.

This is a mayfly. This is a nymph. This is a midge, a caddis fly, a stonefly.

Three steps. Recast. Up to the next hole, around the bend.

The weather holds, bugs hover in the shade, birds rise and soar, a leaf floats downstream and comes to rest in the film. Cottonwoods sway in the breeze. We turn to the water and embrace the blindness. Our senses come alive—sight, hearing, touch, but most of all the sense of joy we feel when a fish bites. At night, the stars align; by day the sky is calm, the water clear. We go through the motions, picture the face of a clock as we cast on a lake, count to five, ten, fifteen or work an extended drift on a river, because there might be a fish in there.

11. Autumn Splendor

WHERE DOES THE TIME go? For months, summer drags on, the air close and hot, earth scorched, creeks dry, the mercury hovering around 115 in a burning valley of creosote and prickly pear by day, bright lights of suburban sprawl by night: strip malls, chain restaurants, every day the same, every other weekend an exodus to higher ground, to cool mountain air. The time between trips spent shuffling gear, tying flies and working my day job, until another summer has rolled by and I need to get moving.

In September the high-country air has a bite, the summer hatches tail off and hoppers are on the menu. They shoot across the meadow as you walk to the stream. Those waning days of summer, the days shorter, when sunflowers whither and the bush flares in red and yellow, when storms come and go. At night, an elk bugles and the clouds break and drift away. Shooting stars flash and Orion wheels between a gap in the trees and I fall asleep, wake before sunrise, listen to the water, an owl's hoot. Fog has settled over the valley. That bull calls from somewhere distant, still at it, the horny bastard.

By October I'm ready to ditch work, flee the city, and live on the road. The truck becomes a moving base camp for two weeks of fishing and backpacking, maybe a few days of hunting, the camper shell stuffed with gear—clothes, food, coffeepot, stove, rods, reels, waders, fly boxes, backpack, firewood, books and maps, gewgaws and skyhooks. Two weeks without email, memos, or other forms of digital bondage, the cell service spotty, stars bright, days cool, the future unclear.

I'm convinced that a lot of anglers live in metaphorical deserts—urban centers far from the nearest trout stream. The rent gets paid, the job comes with health insurance, a 401(k) match, with enough left over for gas and a fly rod once in a while, so they stay. Somewhere along the line, they acquire things, take on responsibilities—kids, dogs, a mortgage.

From time to time, they get lost in this daydream about a little place in the woods, not ten minutes from a trout stream, look into the cost of high-country real estate during their lunch break, and find a shabby lineup of starter homes that list for more than half a million bucks, fixer-uppers with good bones. Something is off here, but there's not much the average angler can do about it, so we soldier on.

The Western economy has changed in the last few decades, and anglers, hikers, ski bums, and other fun hogs have driven that change. A lot of us technically come as tourists, flatlanders and urban voyeurs who drop by during the summer, but our money remains a critical part of the glue that binds this economy. We buy food, gas, tackle. We hire guides and sleep in hotels, feed the beast, an outdoor industry that studies indicate has grown into a trillion-dollar enterprise. Show up late and you'll hit the off season, that time between leaf peeping and snowboarding, when restaurants shut down for a few weeks and the help gets out for some serious hiking.

Autumn is a farewell to high-country fishing. Soon blizzards will blow in from the mountains, the roads buried, lakes frozen, nights so cold that trees snap. The days get shorter, a grim reminder of the days I've squandered. Time to fish, to walk, to *be*.

The march of time as aspens yellow and geese cackle. The forest sheds its skin and fades to brown and gray until a pallor hangs over the woods. Snow falls, skeins of ducks move, and you sense the long sleep that lies around the corner—bone-white aspens, icy lakeshores, cold as a knife. McGuane writes that "Fall gives us a vague feeling that the end of everything is at hand," and it *does* feel like that, but it's not the end, it's just a break in the action, a few months of waiting for another spring summer fall of trout fishing.

The tailwater remains a pivotal part of these adventures, a homecoming, a chance to anchor one part of the trip to big fish that feed all day. Hours pass, casting and mending, the blur of thrashing rainbows, until darkness pushes me off the water and I set up camp, satisfied the trip is going well—dinner finished or on the way, waders flung over the camper shell to dry. Bugs circle the lantern. The day has passed quickly, with lots of fish caught on tiny flies, a sense that everything in the world is connected, the universe wrapped around fishing in ways we can't explain, and I want my thoughts to rise to the moment. But it's late, the mind wanders and drifts downstream.

In time I leave the tailwater for more intimate streams, or go to slickrock, shoulder a pack and head into the high desert for a change of scene. Pots and pans clang as the truck bounces on another gravel road. Sometimes I stop to shuffle and rearrange gear, offload the trash, and get ready to check out another stream, for there's a lot of water out there, more than one person can fish in a lifetime. You do what you can.

It's good to be on the road—all those browns that you hold and release, the hope of bigger fish, of days grand and glorious, though in reality the woods are getting ready for their long sleep.

At some point you have to think about what day it is. Things that seemed important a week ago are all but forgotten. You've hit the sweet spot when time shifts enough that you lose track of it.

And before you know it, you're headed home, a tank full of gas, a head full of memories, camera full of moments. Maybe you've ridden out a storm or two, and maybe things haven't gone quite as planned, but that's all right. You don't want to go back to work, to this other life of screens and flashing lights, of go-go, buy and buy and buy, but on balance it's a good life, so you brace yourself.

By the time winter comes, I'm grateful for everything: grateful I had an opportunity to get in those last days, grateful that I live in the desert. Winters are mild here, and you can fish year-round if you put your mind to it, but I've never fully taken advantage of that because I have bird dogs who rule the household during hunting season. The days are packed.

Some people see Phoenix as nothing but metal, glass, and concrete, a sea of humanity in the desert. I see the hub of a wheel, a geography that reaches into southern deserts, eastern mountains, north into the Colorado Plateau, places with trout in the creases, a few bass. I like it here.

And I'm not the only person who follows this lopsided calendar, this rhythm of seasons. A local fly shop owner used to chase quail and deer in the winter and trout in the summer. The writer E. Donnall Thomas Jr. winters in Arizona. Doug Peacock winters here. We have thousands of snowbirds from Canada, and my guess is that some of them fish on their way down. I stick around, still here when the going gets hot.

The dog has grown old, no pup is in the wings, and I'm in the autumn of my years, maps etched into my brainpan, the winter of old age somewhere ahead, but this list of places I want to *be* keeps rolling through my mind. There are nice browns in the hills, trying to fatten up for the winter, birds in the field. Ducks will arrive soon. Good God, I have a lot to do.

Fishing offers us a shot at leaving the desert, the physical and the metaphorical. It's a journey, a series of road trips, of walks out the door into this other world where trout are the focal point, and the West's far-flung corners are a bonus. Every fall I go through this transition, from the drudgery of summer to cooler days. Background noise fills my head as I go through the mental gymnastics of wondering whether I should move to a cooler climate. By mid-December, that thought vanishes because it's cold as hell up there, though I will allow that my last visit was worth the trip.

Autumn. The hellfire days of summer gone, frost coming to the high country, the wet, muddy days of spring months away. Miles of blacktop and gravel, fish netted, the fly shops with their rows of tiny midges, their big streamers. The best moments of autumn are fleeting. Photos do not quite capture them and our stories fall short. A pulse beats beneath everything, and colors flash as you pass under a canopy of trees, stand by the river and sort through your fly boxes. Red. Yellow. Brown. Another year passes. The land sheds its skin. Shall we drive?

Part II
On the Road

12. A Hundred Fish

CLIFFS TOWERED ABOVE, SMALLMOUTH fed below, and the day got better with every cast. Jason and I fished woolly buggers with rubber legs and lots of lead. Fran fished a nymph. It didn't matter.

The Red River snakes through the rough hills of eastern Arizona, with feeder creeks and side canyons spilling in along the way. Skinny dirt trails lead from rim to river, vanish into boulder fields, willow thickets, and bramble. Miles come hard on the Red, where you must pay attention to every step, eyes peeled for rattlesnakes or agave spikes, but a great fishing hole could be right around the corner. So you walk, and you walk, until you get tired of walking. Then you fish.

I saw my first bear on this river. I had hiked in with my dog, a barrel-chested German Shorthaired Pointer bitch with a stubby tail, made camp under a cluster of bent oaks, rose early, crossed the river, and caught a couple of nice bronzebacks out of a deep pool. It was mid-morning on a summer day, and a sound fluttered above the trees—a soft clang, a metallic note. I stopped to listen and heard nothing but wind and water, so I kept fishing.

A loud splash. A black bear swimming across the pool. He climbed out and shook himself, fur rippling from shoulder to haunch. Water sprayed in sunlight. I grabbed my gear, whispered to the dog, and eased away. The bear walked along the stream toward me, stepped into a thicket, and vanished.

We crossed the river to see what was left of camp, where the bear had gnawed and pillaged: the tent rumpled like green and white sheets, poles splayed, sleeping bag in a heap and torn in a couple of places; a foam rubber mattress dragged into the bushes, a corner eaten, some pieces of it just gone. My pots and pans, clean and off the ground when I left, lying in dirt and juniper berries. My food still hung from a tree.

I caught a couple more fish, gathered my gear, and hiked out, my boots sloshing with river water, the top of my pack lopsided where the bear tore it.

Back then the workdays passed in ten-hour shifts on the copy desk of a suburban daily—a couple decades before news was free, then fake, the whole world up for grabs. I worked, chased girls, drank beer, my dreams out of reach. But I did go back to the river at every opportunity. I studied topo maps in hopes that the fishing would be better far from the road, and it usually worked out. We bumped along the gravel, then dirt two-tracks, parked at the canyon's edge, and walked a mile or two before wetting a line, making camp on dusty benches or sandy flats. Or we car camped on the rim, dropping down to the river to fish.

A few memories from those days have broken off and burrowed deep: Joe standing on a bend in a river singing a Jimmy Buffett song about a bear and moonshine, the shorthairs swimming, buckets of crawdads, big fish, bears and turkeys, flashes of whitetail deer, driving up in the dark, sitting on the tailgate, and watching a meteor shower. Stout juniper trees, shady groves of oak, tall ponderosas.

My life changed over time, the inevitable and unconscious changes that come with age, choices made and unmade, time passing and events unspooling behind the scenes. I got married and divorced, took out a mortgage on a suburban home. Watched the local economy soar, then crash. But the Red sparked an obsession with wild ground I couldn't shake. I took up fly-fishing and started releasing fish. I traveled all over the Southwest, hiking, fishing, and rambling around Indian ruins, ghost towns, and trout streams, blank spots on the map.

Changes were on the horizon. Bobbers became strike indicators. This seemed harmless enough, but other changes were afoot, such as the polar ice caps melting because of the world's energy cravings. We could look this up on our phones, which needed electricity. Reservoirs dropped, Phoenix nights grew warmer, walls of dust blew up from the south, wildfires consumed the ponderosa forest, and streams filled with ash—including one of my favorite trout streams. The fish have since recovered, but the fire gave us a glimpse at the new reality. Water is scarce in the Southwest, so losing a stream for a few years is a big deal.

Out in the mountains the volcanoes have fallen silent. Plates shift, peaks rise or wear down, the streams formed by the slow grind of geology—water cutting down, stone heaving upward. Days on the river pass and memories settle into the hippocampus: miles of new water, base camps, and juniper smoke. A bouncy drive. We shoulder packs, cross the river a couple of times, until we camp on a sandy beach, catch a few fish. The cinnamon bear that walked by our camp and glared at us. I may have pissed him off.

I had packed an air horn, on the theory that the noise would run a bear off, should one come around. Turns out you only need to blast the thing once. The bear turned tail and ran from the sound like a runaway cement truck. I talked trash, told him to move along, but I couldn't leave it at that. I blasted that stupid horn again, and this time he slammed on the brakes, came to a stop, sauntered into the woods. About five minutes later, he walked by at a leisurely pace in the trees, upslope from our camp, and gave us the stink eye. Yes, that's an anthropomorphic interpretation, but trust me, mister bear was pissed.

We kept a few fish and cooked them for lunch after the hike out—golden brown fillets, served with a side of fresh pineapple. A year later a wildfire took out more than half a million acres of Arizona forest. Word spread, like that fire. Summer rains in the aftermath of the fire carried mud and ash into the watershed. Most of the fish were gone. It would take time for them to recover. I had things to do, so I did them, but it seemed odd to leave the Red out of the rotation.

———

Years after the fire, Jason, Jill, Fran, and I met for a trip to the Red. After a few hours of gravel and boulder crawling, we spilled out of the truck, fiddled with our packs, and started downhill, passing a few fishermen walking up the trail. Two dragged stringers of smallmouth gleaming in sunlight. We asked them about the fishing, but they had difficulty forming complete sentences. All they could say was "a hundred fish, a hundred fish, a hundred fish." The river sang below, the trail splayed out onto the banks, and we moved downstream along a flat stretch of dirt and sand until boulders and willows choked it off. But boulder-hopping got old in a hurry, and after a while we turned back to a sandy shelf we had passed earlier, the one with dark sand, a few tent spots, piles of bear shit.

We dropped packs and started fishing. Most of the fish were small, but it took the edge off the drive and set the tone. When the sun got low everyone gathered wood in the gloom, and as dusk bled away to dark, a fire burned, the tents pitched, our gear scattered in piles. Cairns marked the way to the bear bags. We cooked burritos in the coals, sipped beer and wine, and told stories.

The next morning Jason and I pushed downstream. We wanted to cover a few miles, see some new ground, but temptation got the best of us. We started to fish within ten or fifteen minutes at a deep pool.

At first it was a fish here and there, nothing to get excited about, but they started to add up, and it kept getting better until we caught fish with every other cast.

Smallmouth strike hard and fight well. I used to fish with a guy who used a strike indicator on the Red, but I don't use one. I watch the end of my fly line and set the hook for any pause or twitch if I'm dead drifting, but a lot of times I just strip line, the strike an all-out assault at the end of the swing. If you miss that, you don't need an indicator, you need to see a doctor.

Catching smallmouth is a nice break from the delicate nuances of trout fishing—fine tippet, fussy fish, sparse hatches, teeny flies, and stealth. I like to fish a clear line, no heavier than eight-pound test, but that's about as stealthy as I get. These fish eat crawdads and love hellgrammites, so I usually fish a woolly bugger. For the last decade or so, I've added lead eyes and rubber legs, but any pattern that looks something like a crawdad or hellgrammite will work. Size BB split shot helps get the fly deep if the bite is slow. Once in a while, they'll take a hopper, damsel, or popper. I once caught a twenty-inch fish with a Dahlberg diver on the surface.

We cast again and again, and the fish kept coming. At some point, I took a piece of cord out of my pocket and strung one up. When Fran caught up to us, I already had three or four. He had a hot fly and started to add fish, including a nice chubby one. We worked a hole about two hundred yards long, cast after cast, fish after fish. I hadn't caught that many fish on the Red in years. It was a lot like the old days, standing in a river, water up to your thighs, the fish feeding in a frenzy. They came in twos and threes, boiling up from boulder piles seen and unseen. A dozen. Two dozen. Fran said later he caught two while untangling his line, the fly sinking out there in the water. I caught fish on the swing, on dead drifts, stripping, and daydreaming. I would lift my rod to recast and a fish was on. Four dozen. More.

A hundred fish.

The truth is I have no idea how many fish we caught—and don't care. We didn't talk much because words, like numbers, fail on such days. Morning passed. We got back to camp for a late lunch, lolled around in the sun, packed our stuff, and headed up the hill. Fran and I took turns lugging the stringer, which was wrapped around a driftwood handle. By the time we got to the truck we had switched to a bigger handle so we could carry the fish up together, one person on each side. It would be about midnight before we got home and took up the fillet knife.

There was no going back. I was older and had moved on from my suburban daily gig to a metro daily gig I was about to lose. But I had established a routine—work all week, roam the backcountry on weekends, and it stuck. Not much had changed. The roads were a mess, and the walk was a slog.

Our lives pass quickly on this planet, which is shaped by forces bigger than us, forces we try to explain with our gods, our geological ages, our poems and songs and stories, our cycles of life, our studies in chaos and complexity. We build empires, which fall. We have children, each generation an immortal force that unspools in a few decades yet leaves behind another generation. It's too much for the human mind to grasp because answers raise new questions, and so we simplify, lose ourselves in the here and now, the empirical, the tactile.

A lover's touch. Food and drink. A walk up a mountain. A hike into a red canyon on a sunny day. At night the rods lean against a bush, the fly boxes stuffed with woolly buggers. The moon is down, the bear bags hung, the fish are out there, and tomorrow's another day. The coals burn red, stars shine above, and all we hear is the river.

13. Rock 'n' Roll Hill

ONE OF MY FAVORITE places to fish lies off a rimrock point in eastern Arizona. It takes about four hours to get there, the final push a place called Rock 'n' Roll Hill, where the road rises over a bouldered slope, snakes through alligator junipers and yellow grass, then bowling ball-sized boulders, until at last you park in a clearing that overlooks the stream. You can still go there and have the place to yourself. I cracked an oil pan there once. I wasn't happy about that, but beat up trucks are one of the costs of doing business in the backcountry.

Some of my favorite places to fish have somehow survived the internet, population growth, GPS, fresh pavement, the flotsam of modern life that can ruin a good stream. They have survived fishing writers, careless chat room name-drops, and other foolishness. One reason for this, to paraphrase Tim Wu, is that our culture places a high value on convenience: People want everything and they want it now.

Wu is onto something. The tyranny of convenience trumps everything in our culture. Fly-fishing goes against the grain with its time-consuming rituals—pulling on waters, stringing up the rod, staring at your fly box, the fingers tugging at various knots, the cast. You're there to catch fish, but there are no guarantees, and so you learn to embrace the calm and the quiet.

Before these rituals comes the drive, tires purring on asphalt, the Great American Road Trip. We hear nothing but the engine's drone, maybe the radio, the chatter of a fishing buddy. We taste nothing but road food—salty, greasy, or sweet, the sun pounding on the windshield, the air conditioning brushing against our skin. We fill the tank and we're off, looking for the gravel turnoff, and the one after that, until at last we arrive at that lake or stream.

The drive is ritual, the drive is therapy, the drive is long and monotonous.

You stock up on mandatory supplies—gas, water, coffee, food—leave town in morning light and think about everything in general and nothing particular. You daydream about fishing. Even an early start comes with no guarantees, because a lot of things can slow you down: lunch, license, ice, gas, hat, sunglasses, wrong turns, dead batteries, and flat tires. Outside of music, the only things that can make a drive seem shorter are a dog, a fishing buddy, spouse, or girlfriend who wants to be there.

The closest we come to bowing to the tyranny of convenience is fishing closer to home. Nothing wrong with that. Sometimes it works out surprisingly well, but sometimes you get what you pay for: crowded water and slow fishing.

Bad roads serve as gatekeepers that keep out the riffraff, even in the age of the internet. Especially in the age of the internet. Washboard gravel that goes on forever. Roads that unspool into white-knuckled boulder crawls, cobbled swales, hardpan, and clay, roads you talk about years later, some on the map, some not, some that split or meander, no signs, no water in sight, so your trip becomes an act of faith, not fishing, not hiking, not anything, just wandering across gravel and dirt. Backcountry wisdom holds that the rougher the road, the better the fishing, so you bounce along, creep over rocks, blast through mud, checking and rechecking the map. It takes a little extra time, the right attitude, patience. A good truck is a must.

James Babb once wrote that the automobile tops his list of the most important innovations in fishing. We take driving for granted, but most of us wouldn't do much fishing if we had to load up all our fancy tackle on a mule. Jen Corrinne Brown writes that the auto had a major impact on western waters, bringing tourists and their appetites, their fishing gear, their Kodaks, their families, beginning a tradition based on various portions of reality, myth, beauty, hatchery magic, and marketing. Few of us live on a trout stream, and so we gas up and drive, polluting the air to enjoy nature, but life is full of contradictions. It's messy and never exactly how you want it.

You can still go to one of my favorite lakes and have the whole place to yourself. Not likely, but possible. You can get there a couple of ways. One route passes well-worn roads, the beaten path that most anglers take on their way to various lakes or streams. The other snakes through a backcountry labyrinth, an old forest of oak and pine that rises up to aspen and coniferous hill country. Either way, it takes you a good while to get there. So it was a nice surprise to go there a while back to find the place all but deserted. A couple of guys in kick boats worked the far end, and we camped where the lake shallowed against the trees. The fishermen took off and we had the place to ourselves. We didn't catch many fish, but we had a nice night, the stars bright, the lake glass, the browns hunkered down.

One day Cinda Howard and I drove back from a fishing trip when I said something about the Red. She said she had never fished the lower section, mostly because she never took the time to figure out the various access points. She has spent decades fishing in the Arizona high country and has it dialed in so well that she guides for a living. But she left off about sixty miles of good water, all because of the roads. It occurred to me that I had spent half my life exploring that river, though I'm not crazy about the drive. My first time there I drove a Mustang, the hatchback model they made in the late '70s. After a few years I sold the car and began a journey of more than half a million miles, driving a pickup, a Jeep Cherokee, another pickup, and the pickup I'm driving now.

I fished off of Rock 'n' Roll Hill for years. Later I branched off to other access points, map reading and wayfaring, but eventually I moved on to other streams and other states, as that thing called life kept tugging at my sleeve, nudging me here, there, drawing me to new water. Time passed.

Not long ago I went back, and nothing much had changed. I had to backtrack and study the map a few minutes to make the final turn, but at some point instinct took over, as if all those trips had woven hill and valley into my DNA. I drove through fields of sunflowers and pine until at last I reached the boulder-strewn slope of Rock 'n' Roll Hill and started up, leveled off, and crawled past the thick juniper trees, the road as nasty now as it was twenty-five years ago, the trail just as sketchy.

There was never much of a trail to the river. You can pick one up from the bottom, or the top, but it fades in the middle, and you make your way through the rocks the best you can. From a distance, these routes look impassible, like cliff bands that wrap around high hills, but up close they play out gradually, just rocky slopes that allow safe passage, and this one was no exception.

The river had changed, but not much. Runoff had blown out a major logjam, for example, and a few sandbars had shifted, but the river flowed, shallow then deep, more or less as I remembered it—holes spaced out about a quarter mile apart, thin trails through the willows, bouldered passages, various stream crossings. By late afternoon I had made my way to a bend, where one of my favorite camps on the river had grown over from lack of use, the log benches either broken up for firewood or washed away. I had brought several friends there over the years, but all that remained was a fire ring. Willows crowded the banks in a few places, and getting a cast off was tricky, but the hole wrapped around a bend for about two hundred yards. It was deep, rocky, and full of fish.

That was a nice surprise in an age when so many stories of rivers are stories of loss. I was happy the camps weren't trashed, but I wouldn't have minded if they got used once in a while. The fact that they weren't says something, though I'm not sure what. I think the new generation of backpackers walks trails, not wild rivers. Or maybe they don't like to drive the back roads. Which brings us back to Wu's tyranny of convenience.

The shrinking attention span, the need for convenience, may be changing how people travel, how they fish, how they view life in general. Short of more pavement, higher speed limits, faster trucks or teleporting, it seems unlikely we're going to make long drives into short ones any time soon.

So Rock 'n' Roll Hill was just as I remembered it, and the fishing was good. I started back to the truck but stopped at one last pool before heading up the hill. The fish had started to go crazy over a caddis hatch, and I couldn't pass that up—catching smallmouth on dries. By the time I started moving again, the light had dimmed. A rattlesnake writhed in the brush at my feet and set my nerves on edge. I thought I would cross the river and shoot up to the truck, but it took longer than I thought, and before I knew it daylight faded away to dark. For a time, I flailed away in the rimrock, the dog walking behind me, a bit confused. The headlamp came out as we went back down, the night creatures stirring—a skunk flashing white, a couple of raccoons in the trees across the river, eyes aglow, until we had retraced our steps. Luke took the lead, nose to the ground and on trail. He had picked up our scent and was tired of following an idiot.

The next day the fishing was decent—not the best ever but good enough, and we headed out around lunchtime, the drive down the hill slow and bouncy. At one point, a young cinnamon bear ran by, scampered up a ponderosa. I left with a sense that I had stayed away too long. Sure, that last stretch of road looks nasty, but the place was just as I imagined—willing fish, no crowds, nice weather. I'm sure I'll be back. It's beautiful out there, and the drive is nice.

14. Bends

I DON'T REMEMBER MUCH about the trip. We took the Beeline Highway, which snakes out of Phoenix and into the Sonoran Desert, through hills that green up with winter rain and fade to pale yellow by midsummer. Tourists haul boats and campers up the Beeline each weekend, especially during the summer, when they want to flee the desert heat. They stuff their truck beds with camping gear, grills and coolers lashed tight, plastic bags flapping in the wind: anglers, hunters, yuppie hikers, harried suburbanites and their spouses, the back seats crowded with kids and sleeping dogs, engines racing as the highway climbs higher until they leave the desert behind.

It was November, late in the day, and by nightfall we had reached the high country, headlights cutting through the dark. The time had passed in the usual chatter that kicks off any road trip: dregs of the workweek, life in the city, the big rainbow trout in our future. We had booked a float trip with a guide on the San Juan, and all we had to do to catch these fish was get there, show up at the fly shop, step into the boat.

An elk stood on a bend in the road, a midsized bull, facing left, moving slowly. But in a flash it whirled around and ran in front of us, and the next few seconds played out in slow motion: Hitting the brakes, yelling and screaming as we swerved, tires screeching, the great brown body lifting off the pavement when we made contact, the pause that followed, how it dropped on the windshield, stayed there half a second and vanished. I heard it roll over the luggage rack as Jill fought for control of the Xterra until it came to a stop.

Stepping out into the November chill, steam rising from the wreckage, engine fluids bleeding onto blacktop. The point of impact, concave of the radiator, the twisted metal. I imagined that a mountain of paperwork stood between us and the river—insurance agents, adjusters, pencil pushers, thick books of rules and regulations to negotiate. Our fishing trip was over.

People pulled over to help. Jill said she had killed an elk, tearfully, and without a thought of ourselves. At one point, I saw a light brown shape by the road, but I spoke of this to no one. When I looked again, it was gone. Someone called the authorities on a cell phone. People asked: Where is the elk? We pointed back, into the darkness. A few bits of fur blew in the road. Four points of a rack had broken off and lay on the shoulder. Scratches marked the spot where his hooves left the pavement.

A state trooper arrived and the paperwork began. A young man named Trevor had stopped to see if he could help. He had spent most of the day archery elk hunting, then took his coon dogs out for a spin. We talked. Out of earshot of Jill, he said an elk can go a long way when adrenaline takes over, on three legs if it has to. We walked alongside the road, up a gentle slope and back down, until my flashlight came to rest on a bull elk lying in the rocks.

In Arizona, motorists can claim the meat of game animals they hit with trucks or cars, but we had no way to bring those elk steaks to the freezer. Trevor offered to drop off his dogs and come back, help butcher it, and hang it at his place for a day. I did the math and we were left with this: When the butchering was done, I would be stranded somewhere without transportation. He didn't say it, but I guessed that his willingness to help would end about the time he needed to get back to the field for his own elk. A tow truck would arrive soon, and unless we had some other way to get around, we would have to get on it. We had calls to make, a drift boat trip to cancel. So we signed the carcass over to a group that feeds the poor, rode down the Rim in the tow truck.

Sleep came in fits. I would close my eyes and picture the side of that bull, the crash of first impact, the forever pause as he left his feet, another crash as he hit the windshield, the shattered glass that somehow held together in a thousand little pieces, the banging against the luggage rack, fluttering thoughts of mortality, until I drifted off, only to wake up, close my eyes, and see the same images play over and over.

In the morning we learned no adjuster would come that day, or the next. No adjuster would come for two weeks. We had no mountain of paperwork and could not find a place to rent a car. We made phone calls. Dave came up and gave me a ride back to my truck in Phoenix, and by nightfall we were back on the road, going fishing—what anyone with any sense would do, given a few days off work and a second chance at life. We got as far as Gallup, which looks rough around the edges, but is surrounded by high desert buttes, endless mesas, red horizons made for the silver screen, and we spent a night at a hotel known for its famous guests: Doris Day, Humphrey Bogart, Jack Benny, Jimmy Stewart, Kirk Douglas, Lucille Ball, and so on.

When we got on the water the next day, a fierce wind whipped through the canyon. We are taught from the day we pick up a fly rod how to deal with wind, and a skilled or determined flycaster can fish through a few gusts or a stiff breeze. But when wind blows so hard that bugs don't hatch, fish don't bite, indicators move sideways, and you can barely tie knots, the ability to flop a fly into the current doesn't mean much. I pushed on without a bite. We had come all this way. Now this.

Rick Hooley hobbled about as he got the boat ready at Texas Hole. He had hurt himself deer hunting in Nebraska with Tim Chavez, owner of Abe's fly shop/motel/restaurant/guide service, which at the time was an institution on the San Juan. Chavez told us about it at the shop. Something about a tree or a tree stand. How Hooley had called on the radio in a lot of pain. How the radio went dead.

On the way to the water, Hooley shrugged and said the doctors had scheduled an MRI for the next day. He said the bite was slow, and we might have to work for our fish. The guides start their float trips at Texas Hole, with its riffles and braids, its deep channel, easy access, boat ramp, fast runs, and slow eddies. Biologists say it holds thousands of trout.

Hooley was right—we would have to work for our fish, but we caught them. We took a few at Texas Hole and worked downstream, and as we did, the sky turned gray, the clouds grew dark, rain jackets came out, and it started to snow. Our hands got cold and fish stopped biting for a time. A few flurries whipped across the river, and we kept moving, casting, netting a fish or two, pulling up anchor, hoping for something better around the next bend.

My feet got cold, Jill's hands got cold, and Hooley's leg hurt, but it's easy to shrug off pain and bad weather when you catch fish. We ate lunch on a bench overlooking the river, got back to fishing because it was too cold to sit around, and waded on a broad flat where I cast to risers sipping mayflies. Hooley hobbled around and had Jill throw nymphs. We stepped out to fish the Lower Flats for a time, then floated by some pools and pockets that can be tough to wade, places around Lunker Alley and Baetis Bend.

One thing I've learned from fishing with Hooley is to tie big knots. It's faster than squinting over a small loop of tippet. His double surgeons knot made a loop about the size of a baseball, with tag ends three or four inches long. He moved the weight and strike indicator often, explaining how the fish move from one stage of a hatch to the next as the day passes: larva, pupa, emerger. He fished eggs because, well, it was November, and eggs work in November. He fished midge larvae, foam winged emergers, and said it's hard to go wrong with a sparkle dun during the *Baetis* hatch. In slow water, fish feed early, worms work where the river bottom is muddy, and so on. I learned a lot fishing with him.

I wish I could point to a moment that defined the day, a hot streak or a big fish, but there wasn't one. Somewhere upstream from Baetis Bend, I got into a good rainbow that slammed the fly and dove for the bottom. I fought it awhile, but in the end it got away. We caught fish all day, so we were not left with a moment but with many moments. In short, a perfect day. We learned a little about fishing the river and had a great time. The clouds broke as we worked our way downstream. When we got off the water, the sun was shining.

In the morning I fished a little, and we got ready to go. We took a walk to look at some Pueblo rock art Hooley had pointed out from the boat, then headed home, past New Mexican badlands, the Navajo Nation, Gallup, down to the Rim, and I slowed the truck far more than necessary when an elk's rump slipped into the trees along the highway. I called Hooley not long after this. His leg? Fractured. He sat at home in a cast. The insurance company dragged its feet for weeks and finally decided to fix Jill's Xterra. The whole process took three months.

We complained about the usual things as the holidays approached. We scribbled out Christmas cards, shuffled through crowds and bought stuff, fueling the economy's holiday push. When a local fly-fishing club had its Christmas banquet, I dropped some money on raffle tickets, threw most of them into a cup for another half-priced float trip with Rick Hooley. And I won. For the second year in a row, I won.

The desert stayed warm for a while, but rain and snow were not far off. We had what passes for winter in the Sonoran Desert. Dave and I walked the southern Arizona hills for Mearns quail. Relatives started to pour in to escape the cold, and the holidays shaped up as they often do. Bills piled up and work piled up at the office. I thought about the good Samaritans who stopped to help, Hooley at home in his cast, days on the river, and people down on their luck passing around a platter of elk.

We were lucky to be alive, left to ponder a few simple truths—that accidents happen, seatbelts work, people care, but also that our lives are often shaped by what we cannot see or control, the things that lie around the bends. The unexpected elk, a big fish, unexplored water, fate, death, the kindness of strangers. So we start the truck and drive, up the Beeline and through the pines. We lift anchor and push off to see what happens next, cast and mend over deep pools. We lay our money down for raffle tickets, deer tags, a hot fly at the shop. We take our chances and keep moving. We follow the river, though the river cares nothing for our needs, into new water and old, into red canyons or long valleys, until the end of our days.

15. Magic Bug

RACCOONS CAME OUT OF the darkness into the lantern's glow, about half a dozen of various sizes. They lingered as if waiting for a handout—climbing trees, ambling by slowly, until I shooed them away. I was camped by the San Juan River. August, the nights warm, the crickets singing, the river corridor alive with blue herons, deer, frogs, coyotes, and cottontails.

The fish at the San Juan grow shoulders and get selective. You can spend an hour or two casting to a bunch of feeding trout, all because you spotted a nice riser at the head of a pool. It gets kind of addictive. You cast, cast again. Spot another fish, and another after that, until your original plan, to walk a half mile to a sweet spot upstream, gets derailed.

But the fishing had been slow, which left me with a choice—stay an extra day or get moving. I had planned to move on, to fish the high country of Colorado and New Mexico, where rivers and creeks with Spanish names tumbled out of granite peaks into broad alpine valleys. Places on maps, both new water and familiar water, places I said I'd fish more if I had the time.

So I stuck with the plan, and the next morning I broke camp, fished for a couple of hours, soaking up sunshine and casting to a group of feeding rainbows. I drank it all in: the trout sipping midges, the drift boats moving by, the guides speaking softly, the fish netted, the cold water, the hatches, and changing light. I landed a couple of rainbows and drove away.

Perhaps I should have stayed. A bad tire forced me to backtrack into town. Roadwork forced me to sit and wait, and by late afternoon I had only gotten as far as Chama. The local streams had dropped so low that the New Mexico Department of Game and Fish had not bothered to stock them, though I didn't know this until I found a cabin on the edge of town, where the owner complained about the drought. I had imagined the trip differently, to say the least.

I suspect that most desk jockeys who plan fishing trips when they're supposed to be working do the same thing. We conjure up mental images of big fish, peaceful water, and sunny days, leave out the nitty-gritty details such as crowded streams, bad weather, car trouble, roadwork, and losing our way. Our mental maps grow dim and foggy, the driving distances compressed, and slow days are not in the brochure. I should have known that a good trip—any kind of trip—begins with a state of mind, and the first rule is to enjoy the ride.

I left Chama and pushed on to a small stream I had heard good reports about, but the fish didn't bite. Then some kid tried to run some cattle away from his camp with a dirt bike, nearly putting me at the wrong end of a small stampede. The bike roared across the meadow, the cattle trotting and about to run, when some wild-eyed fisherman walked up the stream bank, waving a bamboo stick, and they stopped. We all looked at each other—the cattle, the kid, the crazy fisherman, and went our separate ways. The moment went from loud and surreal to a quiet resignation that I probably wasn't going to catch any fish that day.

Firelight stirred in a mountain breeze. I had moved far upstream, where the creek, mere inches wide, looked worse. Cows bawled and the lantern hissed as I moved around camp, cracked a beer, read a book, and thought about the next day of fishing. Surely, it would get better. Anything would be better. When the breeze died and the fire died and the lantern went quiet and the cows stopped bellowing and planes no longer passed overhead, a deep silence fell over the forest. It was the same silence I had come to know in my travels through the high desert. Had it followed me here? It settled across the hills, like clean sheets under a blanket of stars, big and profound and endless. I crawled into my bag and slept.

Morning spilled across the lake, golden and calm, the silence broken as geese honked and I moved gear into the truck. The engine turned and the miles went by quickly, the truck rattling out of aspen and fir and back into the rough juniper hills, down to straight highways that passed miles of farmland and small gritty towns on the arid plain.

I fished the next river on my list, where I went hours without a strike, then finally took a nice brown around lunchtime. And another after that. The fish took big rubber-legged nymphs. After a while I dropped the indicator and took a couple more fish with a short tight line. The day had some promise.

After lunch I started working another section of stream, moving quickly from one hole to the next. I lobbed the nymph into a pool behind a rock the size of a refrigerator, fished the deep bend behind it without a strike. The river spilled into a whitewater flat after that. It looked slippery and unwadeable. It looked like a good place to turn around. As I started back, I pitched the fly behind the refrigerator rock and the line went tight. The rod tip danced.

The fish took line into the water I had just fished, and I worked to control the head, to keep it away from the fast water, trying to strike that delicate balance, tiring the fish without exhausting it, landing it quickly without screwing things up. It came to the surface briefly. A bright flash, another run. Things got ugly when I got it to the net because it didn't quite fit, but after a couple of attempts I got it in, folded up like a tortilla, slippery and bright. I laid the fish against the rod and noted where its nose came to rest, snapped a few photos, and let it go. It was a cutthroat, about twenty inches, and it made my day.

I only caught one more fish, a rainbow that also filled out the net nicely, though it didn't bulge at the seams the way it had when I landed the cut. I found a place to camp, set up a tarp as a light drizzle began, ate chili as it grew dark, while the clouds drifted over mountaintops. The rain could have darkened my mood under other circumstances, but it came slowly, not too cold, no wind, the sound of it soothing after I strung up the tarp, got my camp squared away, and sat down.

All week I had chased something, driving miles across dusty gravel roads, lonesome stretches of blacktop, and it came together at last about the time I stopped chasing daydreams. Clouds spun overhead, rain fell. I settled into a rhythm, the fish bit, and the weather held, other than a few showers, but nothing too serious. For days, I followed rivers, drove around in my waders, a fly rod strung up in the back of the truck, and marked time by streams fished and fish caught and changing light. I ate chili and burritos for days, drank cold beer by a warm fire.

Funny how one day of fishing can change everything. I had also stopped driving so much, had settled into one area, a river and its tributaries, which gave me a sense of place that you miss on the road, a sense that somehow you belong there, not exactly as a local but a tourist with benefits, a pilgrim from the suburban grind.

The river speaks, your soul awakens, your sense of time changes, and you take everything in stride. Maybe the trip goes the way you imagined, but it has also taken on a life of its own, a fishing trip, warts and all: slippery rocks, achy joints, bad casts, a few stretches of not catching anything, and then the flurry when everything comes together. If I think about it, it happens on a lot of trips. A few days on the road and the traveling blues can set in, but they can quickly turn to joy. The switch flips about the time you have to stop and ask yourself what day it is. Wednesday? No, Thursday. Does it matter?

The magic bug kept working as I fished my way home. Some call it a Pat's rubber leg, but I've seen other names. It's a bunch of rubber legs, a few wraps of lead and chenille. I try to keep a few in my fly boxes at all times. I suppose I should have fished it with an indicator, but the trout just grabbed it. I liked that a lot.

On my last day I drove past a turnoff for the San Juan, where raccoons roamed, deer walked, frogs croaked, and crickets sang in the night. I could picture them, the men and women knee-deep in the water, in waders and boots, casting nymphing rigs in short methodical strokes. I could have headed that way, but instead I stopped to fish a freestone river where I spent an afternoon lobbing my new favorite fly into riffles and pools.

When I got home, I penciled in another week of fishing streams with Spanish names, and when the trip rolled around, it went a lot like the first trip, without doubt or angst. It was autumn at the San Juan, a time when mayflies hatch, when the cottonwoods turn and carpet the ground with leaves. I caught fish, though not the way I had in my daydreams.

Summers pass, autumn nights slip by, mammals large and small sometimes roam the edge of camp. Anything can turn your fortune on the water. A cold front. A hatch. A magic bug. Maybe someday I'll learn exactly when to change flies, tactics, or streams. Maybe someday I'll learn to fish, and to live, without complaint.

16. Animals

CHRIST, I'M GETTING OLD. You take each day at full throttle, eyes bright, legs strong, until you notice that somewhere along the line, your vision got blurry and you've lost a step. You buy glasses, do your best to age gracefully, but you get these reminders that things have changed. I had one of those moments one summer morning at camp, as sunlight spilled across the canyon floor, over treetops and boulders along the creek. The usual morning stuff: birdsong, the dogs roaming while I sipped my first cup, while Jason and Jill stirred in their tents, while water rushed behind the willows. Then the pup barked and trotted back into camp. Someone asked what he had barked at, but I had no idea. Something moved through the trees, dark and bleary in the shade.

Large mammal, I said, trying to focus without glasses or caffeine. It slipped quickly into a green thicket, and I went through the list of possibilities in no particular order. Could be an elk, I said. Bear. Cow. I went back to my coffee.

A few minutes later Jason crawled out of the tent and looked at the hillside above camp.

There's a bear up there, looking at us, he said. I walked to the tent, fumbled around for my glasses, and looked up.

Cinnamon colored.

Uh-huh.

We decided it looked more brown than cinnamon. It stood there another thirty seconds and moved on.

We caught a lot of smallmouth on the usual flies in the usual places that day—buggers lobbed into deep holes, the day sunny and all that, but mostly what I remember is that bear and the fact that I couldn't really make out what had moved around camp. Sure, I had glasses and wore them once in a while for distance, but how do you miss a bear?

Fishing connects us with aquatic animals and creates a bond with the natural world. We poke at caddis larva, search for mayfly nymphs under rocks, note the darting of minnows or crawdads and try to imitate their motion with enough skill to fool a fish. The bond creates moments we remember for the rest of our lives. We hold a trout, feel its struggle, see a wild look in its eye that reminds us of something within ourselves, something we lost touch with long ago. Something primal.

"Fishing is a quest for knowledge and wonder as much as a pursuit of fish; it is as much an acquaintance with beavers, dippers and other fishermen as it is the challenge of catching a trout," Schullery writes. "My home river does not always give me her fish, but the blessings of her company are always worth the trip."

Spend a night by a river and you might see a few stars. Spend a week and the bond with Mother Earth gets stronger as you take note of nocturnal rhythms, the migration of birds, the damp morning air. Somehow it all gets under your skin and in your brain in ways that are hard to track or explain. You can talk about your reasons for fishing, beauty and relaxation and physical exercise, but much of what happens out there takes place under the surface and remains after you've left the water. I suspect a lot of anglers don't think about all that, and most of those who do can't put it into words. They know something vital happens on the water, that they'd rather be there than anywhere else—and leave it at that.

Research confirms that those feelings we get in the great

outdoors are real, as real as it gets. Yet our society puts us at odds with nature. We work indoors, play indoors, eat, sleep, and drink indoors, insulated from the animal kingdom in all its forms. It's comfortable but can also be an anemic, lonely existence.

I do my best to mind the wilderness in my backyard, as they say, to nurture it and help it along. Visitors do come off the mountain from time to time: Quail call, hummingbirds feed, gophers dig up the garden, lizards skitter, mockingbirds sing. A peregrine once ate a pigeon in my backyard. A pair of kestrels learned to fly in it. Owls hoot, coyotes yip, roadrunners trot by on some errand. But it has this backdrop of freeway noise and pale night skies, and it's not the same as getting out into the great wide open. And so I drive and look for a place with less racket where beasts roam.

I cast, mend, focus on the fish, but other creatures slip in and out of the narrative. Eagles and herons come to feed, vultures wheel, and blackbirds chatter in reeds and rushes. A skein of mallards peels away in the morning fog, an elk bugles. The chill reaches under my coat, and I want to go back to the tent, curl up in my sleeping bag, but something moves—a few geese, a deer—and I shake the cold, face the day.

I remember bears running or sauntering, a skunk on the porch of a cabin in Greer, an elk that kicked my dog, deer bolting, snorting, a summer of ospreys that soared and whistled, crashed the water and caught fish. Technically they're hawks, but they look like court jesters of the eagle clan. Some folks call them fish eagles.

A couple months after catching those smallmouth, Jason and I shouldered heavy packs and tottered upstream into the mountains of southern Colorado. The hills above us were capped with bald rock and spindled ridgelines where thousands of spruce and fir trees had dropped their needles and stood dead or dying or ready to die. My notes and my memory remain clear on this: the granite switchbacks, a knee-deep crossing, the campfire's warm glow, rice and beans, thin flaky tortillas, starry night, cool morning.

We rested a day, catching brookies, rainbows, and fish that looked like hybrids, and then pushed on the next morning into the dead zone, stepping into shadow and deadfall, over trees that blocked our way. Each breath came in gulps, each step harder than the last as the trail corkscrewed up canyon, past waterfalls and damp sunlit hollows where the trees, at last, were green. A hailstorm slapped us on our way up a narrow chute and soaked me to the bone. When the switchbacks leveled off to a broad valley between granite peaks, we strung up a tarp, changed into dry clothes, and rested until the shivering stopped. We pushed on, over the pass, into the next valley.

The next morning came pale and damp, with mountain sheep coming and going on the trail, ice and slop underfoot, with water tumbling everywhere, and the air getting thin. Around noon we scrambled up to more than fourteen thousand feet and took in the 360-degree view. Back at camp, the local sheep herd got bold, in spite of our best efforts to run them off. They made whiny noises, chased each other around, squealing and bleating. Babies, mama sheep, stocky males strutting about. Sheep everywhere.

Yellowstone National Park is like a zoo without bars. Deer and elk wander the parking lots, bison cross the roads and roll in dust by the highway. Ah, the noble bison, a beast that looks slow but moves quickly, sure-footed and ornery, known to gore tourists. You can see lots of wildlife in the park in a given week. You can also have fun watching people, and what generations of urban living have wrought: a nation of city folk who have cell phones and cameras but don't have enough sense to give bison a wide berth. People who, when they consider wild animals at all, do so in the abstract: cute, fuzzy, pretty, majestic, photo op.

One year a group of us spent a few days in the park and drove to Soda Butte Creek, if memory serves. When I saw some bison in a meadow along the road, I pulled over, broadside to the animals, screwed a big lens on my camera, elbows propped on the hood for support. My friends pulled up behind me and followed suit. We were careful to keep our distance, the vehicles between us and the beasts, but some tourists pulled over, stepped out of their cars, and a few of them started to approach the bison. One member of our group, P. K. Weis, was a photojournalist from Tucson. We watched the tourists wander toward the bison, and P. K. started to talk about the difference between fine art photography and photojournalism. The artist tries to get the tight shot, he said—a few shaggy curls, the grain of a bison horn bathed in sunlight, and all that. The photojournalist waits for the action shot, the blood that comes when the bison gores some blockhead who gets too close.

I once fished the Firehole River, not far from a small herd of bison. Another angler was on the water, about a hundred yards upstream. Everyone minded their own business, and nobody got hurt.

A summer of fishing passes in a blink, and memories stack carelessly somewhere deep in the frontal lobe. A crowded street corner, a short skirt, a long hike, an afternoon nap, the smell of juniper, a bar in Durango. Animals: a gang of sheep in shaggy white coats, the clamor of geese, frogs bleating, squirrels chattering. You toss a piece of oak on the fire, the grain tight, the wood heavy and dense, stir the coals, sit back and relax. Sometimes, life is about learning to live on this earth gracefully, which can be more difficult than you think, but sometimes it's remarkably simple. You sit and wait and something happens.

I remember sitting in a kick boat on a lake in the White Mountains, where a bunch of fly-fishers finned and rowed and caught rainbows and cuts. The fishing had slowed when an osprey dropped and landed with a sploosh and came up with a fish. Everyone cheered.

A young moose rumbles by the tent, hooves thundering, all legs, and ambles off into the hills. Far too often, we anglers focus on those times when the rods bend and fish come to hand. But some of our best moments come on the riverbank, or in bright corners of the forest, when beasts pass and remind us that we, too, are animals walking the earth with others of our kind—elk, fox, wolf. A bear passes in a blur, and the years go by.

17. Coyote

MIKE COULD BE A real smartass. When the doctors told him he had cancer, he said: "Funny, I don't feel like I'm about to die."

We met at the University of Iowa, back when things looked clear, the future bright, when everything was girls and beer and party, party, party: parties by the river with guitars wailing on the back porch until the neighbors complained; parties at a farmhouse outside of town; parties at the old house where they say Kurt Vonnegut used to live; parties on into the night. Now it all blurs together, the best years of our lives.

We kept in touch after we graduated and went into the big world. He had studied photography and was a good shooter, but I don't think he ever worked a day at a magazine or a newspaper, other than a few freelance gigs. He just went to work, and I remember he said something once about climbing the ladder and not stopping until he got to the top. For a while he jumped around, living in Chicago, eastern Nebraska, Mexico City, until he landed in Denver, not far from some of the best trout streams in the country. Like a lot of people, he could get pretty wrapped up in work and didn't get out on the water as much as he would have liked. He had a wife, a son, two girls in school—no time—but we went fishing a few times, and I enjoyed each trip.

The first time we fished at a place the locals call Deckers, a tailwater section of the South Platte, not far from Denver. We picked up a few flies at a local shop and parked by a bridge. Pretty soon

Mike was taking fish on midges while I had a meltdown. The problem started after I took off my vest, heavy with fly boxes and a 35mm camera. The vest slid down the bank and into the water while I fished, and by the time I realized what had happened, a camera lens got soaked and a couple of fly boxes had started to float away. I grabbed the vest and ran after the bobbing Wheatleys, frantic and cursing.

Years later, I would hear Mike's version, not a tragedy but a comedy. In his version, he's fishing and looks up to see a crazy man running up and down the bank, waving his arms and hollering, though all he can hear is the river. That afternoon I got into a good fish that took me to my backing. I slipped and fell, sprang to my feet, the fish still on, which was about as much dignity as the day would allow, because the fish got off anyway. We drove back to his house for dinner with his lovely wife, his two daughters.

After that, we made a couple of trips to the Frying Pan. We showed up sometime after the famous green drake hatch, but we did okay for a couple of drive-by anglers. The Frying Pan can be as technical as any tailwater, but also rewarding, with fat trout that can make it worth getting on a plane and then making the drive. We found a bar in Aspen that we spent so much time in we called it The Office. I don't recall the name, just a few details: historic building, high ceiling. Wooden trim and a giant mirror behind the bar, a decent beer selection, and a couple of empty barstools. Everything we needed.

Life got busy then, and we didn't see each other for a few years. The next thing I knew bad news started to come across the phone lines. Our friend Bruce died after a string of medical problems, Mike's dad died, his wife had left him, one of his daughters died in a rollover accident, and so on. He moved into an apartment, called it his cabin, and got on with life.

"Well, it sucks, but there isn't anything you can do about it," he told me over the phone. The last time I saw him things had started to look up. He had dropped by Phoenix with his new girlfriend to catch the Iowa Hawkeyes in a bowl game. He had a line on some tickets and offered to find me one, but I had already made plans to leave town on game day, so we met for a beer.

"Call me," he said. "I need to get out and play. I need to fish or go bird hunting."

And so I did, but we couldn't work it out. "Later," I said. "We'll make it happen."

A year or two later Dave and I turned the dogs loose to hunt quail in eastern Arizona. The day began with a lot of promise. We got into birds early but couldn't get into any kind of shooting rhythm, missing birds right and left, one after another.

A couple of creeks fingered across a rocky plateau of yellow grass slashed by red canyons, a timeless landscape where hawks soar and coyotes roam and quail live on edge. Mesquite trees stab deep roots along cobble banks, cholla and prickly pear cactus fan out across the valley, rough juniper hills and mountains push up along the horizon. A few deer and herds of javelina roam the creases and folds, as it has always been.

A narrow asphalt road cuts across these flats, as if someone had the idea that it is important to cross timeless landscapes quickly. In the summer, anglers travel this blacktop on their way to fish lakes and streams. Years pass, the land more or less unchanged, the hunters coming and going until their knees or hips give out, leaving them to sit around camp longer and to talk about how it used to be, when you found quail everywhere, when average years were good, good years were outstanding, and we walked without complaint.

Years of drought have made birds scarce, but for some reason we got lucky that day, bumping coveys and singles as we worked our way across the flats. After about an hour of chasing quail, we stood at the grave of a shorthair I had buried in the desert. I took off my hat by a rockpile in the shape of a cross that marked the spot and looked at my watch. Mike's funeral was about to begin.

The story came out in bits and pieces. How Mike got sick and stayed that way for months. How the doctors fiddled around trying to fix him before they figured out he had cancer. A day or two later the doctors cut into him, but it was no use, the stuff had spread everywhere, so they closed him back up and gave him morphine to ease the pain. He died a day or two later. A mutual friend told me about it over the phone. How he saw Mike in the hospital before the operation, how they had watched a Vikings game as if it were just another day. The day Mike died, this mutual friend went downstairs to adjust a dehumidifier. The handle broke, and water flew everywhere, as if someone had played a trick on him. Mike. Thanks, Mike.

We made camp, built a fire, raised a glass of scotch to Mike, and put on steaks. We played Van Morrison, one of Mike's favorites, and Orion turned in the sky. Betelgeuse and Sirius. A cool breeze blew and dogs snored.

Out in the desert, the moon came up, three-quarters full, the grass pale and silver. We said: "What would Mike say in this situation? He'd say, 'I need a beer.'" So we walked over to the cooler and reached into the ice for a cold one. The day kept coming back to us. What happened back there in the bird field? It was as if the birds weren't real, as if our guns had fired blanks. As if someone had played a trick on us. Mike. Mike on the other side, with Gambel, the shorthair buried down the road. Thanks, Mike.

A coyote howled. Not a pack, not a pair going back and forth—just one, an Apache trickster that howled and howled. The stars wheeled and the breeze kept blowing. The cold slipped under our coats occasionally, and the silence grew big and ubiquitous, perhaps cognizant, the darkness eternal. It was easy enough to imagine that we had company, some wandering souls that blew in from other worlds or out of the canyons.

I'm not ready for this. The list of friends who have departed keeps growing. Bruce. Mike. Jamie after that. I remember Jamie's voice booming over the phone after Mike died, as if he stood in the next room and might walk around the corner any moment. We talked about bird hunting, about getting together for some hunt that never took place, because we had all the time in the world. Cancer again.

I'm pretty sure that, given a second chance, they would have fished more and worked less, but we had all this time, see. Why, just yesterday, we drove on down to the river and it was party, party, party—the air damp and close, fireflies flashing while beer flowed and music played on the back porch and, good Christ, a couple of deputies dropped by around midnight to tell us to turn it down. We felt unstoppable in those days. The world was out there, and we'd take our place in it. All we had to do was work hard, follow our dreams, and it would all work out. Just yesterday Mike told me about this ladder he would climb until he reached the top; just yesterday I sat down at the table with his family for dinner, but somehow it all went sideways, and then everything was wrong.

I miss the rain. I miss days of walking without complaint, the dogs racing to the next covey, the news over the phone all good—let's get together soon—the winters gray and rainy, the fish brawny, the future bright. I miss my friends.

The moments when time stops. That pause when dogs go on point, when a fish strikes, a shooting star flashes, when the sun sets, and silence settles over the land. A woman's smile, a kiss. What happens next is fleeting, sometimes messy, never the same. We cannot hold onto these moments. All we can do is make the most of them, remember them, and get on with life. The dogs sleep by the fire, the fields wither, the range goes to dust, people come and go. The way it has always been.

18. Wild Roses

GOD KNOWS HOW FAR I was from camp. Daylight faded to shades of gray, and the river grew opaque. I scanned the ground for diamondbacks and moved quickly while the usual questions banged around in my head: Was that the last bend? Should I cross here? Why do I always do this?

The water, knee-high, the bottom sloped, until I started to bob, waste-deep, then chest deep, toes searching for bottom on gravel and rock. Up the far bank, dripping wet, walking up a moonlit game trail until I couldn't stand it anymore.

I yelled into the night, and Dennis answered. Camp was just over the rise in front of me.

We sat by the fire. I changed into dry clothes and settled in for dinner and some good talk. Another day on the water, sunny and warm, and it was a good day but I have been known to find fault with such days because I fish. The day had passed in long stretches without a bite. The day had passed with missed opportunities, a head shake, and a breakoff—big fish that played me and got under my skin as I sat and warmed myself by the fire. The day had passed in hatches without risers, roots and rocks, the snort of a couple of startled whitetails in the gloom, in moonlit trails, and a blind river crossing until the day had passed.

The first day passed without much fishing: leaving Phoenix on straight and narrow asphalt, climbing Sonoran Desert hill country into thornscrub and pale juniper woodland, on to the red cliffs of the Mogollon Rim. Black shimmering highway, the whine of tires all around us until the asphalt played itself out into gravel and grasslands, gravel and oak, gravel and ponderosa, a plume of dust rising behind us. We reached the trailhead at midday. Sunlight burned on canyon walls, and Dennis moved down the slope to the river wearing an external frame pack. Tall and fit, he walked quickly, crossing the stream when cliffs cut off passage, splashing through the shallows with his dog, Brindle, a wiry mix named for her color.

After a mile or so, canyon walls pinched in, the crossings more frequent. Progress slowed. The bright green pack bobbed up and down in front of me, and I followed it into the bush, at one point following a bit too closely. Wild roses grew in the thickets, magenta flowers abloom. A branch snapped back and lodged a thorn in my noggin.

We found an old fire ring on a ledge above a shallow rapid, dropped packs, strung up rods, and kept walking. Mayflies hovered, caddis fluttered, but the fish did not rise to my flies or take Dennis's spinners, so we wandered upstream, taken in by shadow and light, as the banks changed from dirt to basalt, the ground formed in a long-ago age of steam pots and hissing ground, scorched earth, and fields of lava that bubbled and hardened, the trees planted by giants or river gnomes. We clambered up a rock face, grabbing handholds, stepping around divots, walking into a shallow bowl that overlooked the river.

Back to camp, to a warm fire and talk that lasted into the night.

Dennis has not embraced modern packs, gear or synthetic clothing. He packs whatever food is handy and fishes with an old spinning rod. At the time, he worked as an investigative reporter who chased stories about Arizona—its quirks, its underbelly of corruption, its cast of characters: Mexican border crossers, polygamists and cults, grifters and swindlers, government sloth and malfeasance, drug runners, and wildfire.

We fell asleep to river music, and in the morning we moved camp to a field of grass and Apache plume, pitched tents, hung bear bags, and grabbed our rods. Miles passed quickly with the packs off, the route moving over benches and along cattle trails that cut across bends rather than around them.

An old metal shed leaned in the shade. Years ago someone spray-painted a name on that shed, black letters scrawled over a corrugated panel: Leonard Gregg. If you lived in Arizona in the summer of 2002, you read that name in the papers while the worst fire in state history burned through the high country.

The fire started near Cibecue, a village on the Fort Apache Reservation. Sunlight baked the hills, the dogs looked for shade, and the men rose early to their work on bright and cloudless mornings with no wind. The solstice was coming and the grasses withered, the hillsides browned up, and the land waited for rain while the newspapers talked about a drought that had settled in.

The ground was primed, but no fires came until Gregg set a fire near the Cibecue rodeo grounds and went home. He was a wildland firefighter who lived in Cibecue, and folks knew him as a kind and gentle soul, a bit simple; news reports said he was touched by fetal alcohol syndrome. He did not cause much trouble growing up, but he decided to jump-start the fire season and put a few dollars in his pocket that day.

Fire crews struggled with the Rodeo Fire. Newspaper reports say that three hundred acres burned the first day of the fire. Or maybe it was a thousand acres—accounts vary. The next day it jumped Carrizo Creek and marched up the Mogollon Rim to feed on the ponderosa forest. It grew into a six-mile wall of flame, two hundred feet high or more, burning at two thousand degrees, enough heat to uproot trees and toss them like matchsticks. By day's end it had consumed about fifty thousand acres. It left some places unburned. It roared through other places and moved on or doubled back. The fire fed for days and took strength.

Somewhere in the high country, a Phoenix woman named Valinda Jo Elliott and a friend, Ransford Olmsted, had business in Young, a community in the Tonto Basin, but they missed a turn and wound up on the reservation. They drove until they came to a barricade. The Rodeo Fire was burning out there, and so the tribe put up that barricade to keep people out. But there is something about signs and barricades in the woods—which feel big and lawless and *free*—that crush that sense of freedom. People do not understand that the woods are finite and getting smaller. So they ignore the signs, which are a buzzkill and surely posted for others.

Olmsted and Elliott moved the barricade and drove deeper into tribal lands, ran low on gas, but kept going, hoping to find services, a house, gasoline—anything to end the Long Drive to Nowhere. They ran out of fuel miles from any town, and Olmsted took off on foot the next day to get help. Elliott climbed a hilltop to see if she could get a signal on her phone, dressed in shorts, a tank top, and flip flops, moving deeper into the forest until the trees grew thick and the way back became unclear. By sundown, she was lost in the woods near Chediski Peak. Here too, accounts vary, but a day later or three days later she heard a television helicopter passing overhead and set a signal fire. The TV crew rescued her, but the fire raced up the mountain, the smoke changing from gray to white to black; then it, too, began to feed. When the fires met in the backcountry, firefighters couldn't do anything but get out of the way. The fire had a new name—Rodeo-Chediski—and it roared through reservation and nonreservation lands. Smoke from the blaze could be seen from Phoenix. It did not stop until it had consumed nearly half a million acres.

Years later and miles from the burn, we pushed beyond the shed, walked a couple miles, and started to fish, the day sunny and warm. Dennis tossed spinners, his reel squeaking above the river's hum, and started picking up smallmouth right away. I tossed olive buggers into deep water and got a few bumps, but no fish. On and on it went, until the day got along quickly as we leapfrogged down the river.

Trees crowded the river's edge. The bugger drifted slowly past gnarled roots, my mind drifting with it until the line snapped clean. What kind of fish breaks off 3X tippet in half a second? A big fish. I tied on a new fly and drifted it by the roots again, just in case. Nothing.

We started to fish our way back. I added some split shot, and the extra weight seemed to help. I got into a good fish that flashed briefly in the shallows, but it got off when I tried to get it on the reel.

Dennis started back to camp. He wanted to gather some wood for a fire before it got too dark, but I stayed on the water, stopping at every hole until I caught a few. That should have been enough, but I kept fishing after that and soon the cliffs turned red and shadows grew long, our camp a good two or three miles away. Clusters of mayflies in various sizes hovered at a couple of places on the river. I stopped to fish, but not much happened.

Which is how I wound up racing back to camp in the near dark, until I crossed the river and climbed that hill and hollered. Dennis answered. I settled in, the fire warm, and the talk went into the night. Our plan for the next day was to work the deep pools upstream. Trout water, we thought, the kind of place where browns grow shoulders. Tall ponderosas framed the stars above when the fire died, and the river sang through the night.

In the morning I tied on a nymphing rig and got nothing until I dropped it into a pool of fast water. The indicator paused. I set the hook and a big fish dashed and dived. My heart raced and my mind raced as the fish circled. I kept the line tight, tight, tight, until he came to hand, an eighteen-inch brown. I pushed upstream, crossing often, fishing pools and pockets, and my hands steadied and the butterflies in my belly settled. The fishing was slow for a time until another fish took me around another deep pocket, a real brawler that flopped and finned and thrashed over a shallow slippery stretch of cobble into the next pool. Somehow I stayed with him without falling on my ass. He, too, came to hand—another brown, fatter than the last, an inch or two longer.

The next couple of hours passed in a flurry of smaller trout, three or four fish in each pool. Fly-fishing magazines are full of advice—the best flies, when to fish and where, but it also helps to put in your time. My father used to say that you won't catch anything unless you put a line in the water. My friend Mark Judkins says: "Plan your work and work your plan."

Clouds break and the sun shines. Fish rise or shut down. Roses have thorns. Push on. Maybe you'll come up empty, or maybe a big fish will take its place in your memory beside the ones that got away. The land, too, has memory. You feel it in the spine of a mountain, the bones of old forests, in the hollows and creases of meadow and canyon, the bends of a river, the heart of a fish that struggles for its freedom, until it all swirls in your head and seeps into your soul—moonlit trails, magenta blooms, shadow, and firelight. These are the gifts of rivers.

19. Lake Solitude

HIGH-COUNTRY SUMMERS IN ARIZONA can have a misleading, volatile cast. Hills and valleys come alive with wildflowers, rising trout, cool nights, Scorpius rising in the southern sky. At first it all feels so perfect—nice weather, good fishing, but then the solstice rolls around, and things change. Lakes warm up, wildfires break out like a rash across the state, smoke settles into valleys, and the trout come off their feed.

I had penciled in a couple of weeks of fishing in the White Mountains, working out of a base camp with a tent as big as a house, and though the days passed pleasantly enough and I caught fish, I felt out of sorts, rambling from place to place, chasing time. People said, you should have been here yesterday. Or, you should have been here last week.

Early June does have a lot of upside: long days, lovely nights, a low chance of rain. But somewhere along the line, a switch flips and the heat settles in. It's cool in the mountains, but in the lower elevations the ground broils, and a searing blanket of misery covers the hills, heat that gives rise to much of the state's geography, a map full of references to Lucifer and his domain: Hellsgate, Hell's Half Acre, the Devil's Highway. You catch trout, but things can slow down considerably as the month wears on. You fish more streams. You head for higher elevations and cooler lakes, pray for rain.

We really do have a Devil's Highway, and used to have two. One cuts through a remote part of the Sonoran Desert in southern

Arizona, near the border. The word highway is a misnomer, a bad joke about a lonesome gravel road in a place with few roads. It's one of the hottest places on the planet. Historically, the road served the Hohokam, the O'odham, the Spanish, Mexican vaqueros, American settlers. More of a trail than a road back then, the highway became known as "a route along which people die," Michael Benanav writes.

Today the road is "actually quite safe," he writes, "surprisingly well maintained and no special skills are needed to navigate it." But we live in complicated times. The desert beyond burns like a griddle, full of ankle rollers, mountains, rattlesnakes. Stick to the road with plenty of water and you're good, even if you break down, because, if you can stand the wait, in a couple of hours a Border Patrol agent will come along. Cross the road on foot to pass through the Cabeza Prieta Wilderness, well, that's a different story. Temperatures can exceed 120 degrees in the summer down there. The region has other graves and bone piles, but it's difficult to know for sure how many. Years ago, the refuge manager at Cabeza Prieta told me they found bodies every year. He didn't have the numbers in front of him, but offhand he guessed it was about a half dozen.

Edward Abbey, the cranky Southwest scribe who loved the desert, is buried somewhere in the Cabeza Prieta. Abbey didn't want to die in a hospital, and he didn't want his corpse to rest under a carpet of Bermuda grass in a Tucson graveyard. When his time came, he left the hospital to die at home. His buddies hauled him out to the desert, trucks loaded with food and beer, shovels and picks, Abbey's corpse in a body bag.

The other Devil's Highway once ran north–south, back when Route 66 was known as the Mother Road, the stuff of song and legend. Back then, the US Department of Transportation followed a rigid system of naming highways, and when it built the sixth north–south offshoot from Route 66, they named it 666. The road snakes through the Apache-Sitgreaves National Forests in eastern Arizona, a woodland realm of spruce and fir, oak and pine, and native Apache trout. It winds downhill from one forlorn vista to another, until it drops you into the Sonoran Desert. Some call it the Coronado Trail because the Spaniard supposedly passed that way.

The region was once home to the Navajo and Apache, to Mormon settlers and cattle rustlers, to copper miners, and ranchers. It remains a woodsy backwater of rugged individualism, feral old-timers, tales of black helicopters and alien abductions.

The Bible says the number 666 is the sign of the beast, the Antichrist, and so naturally the highway drew a lot of attention and produced all sorts of local legends: a girl in a white dress who vanished when motorists pulled over, UFOs, packs of demon dogs, creatures of Navajo legend known as skinwalkers. The other thing is that people kept stealing the signs. So the DOT renamed the highway 191. To me, it's still 666, the Devil's Highway, as I suspect it is to a lot of people. One day, some time ago, I drove a section of it to a small alpine lake.

I had the place to myself—all two or three acres of it—which I didn't expect. A lake that small can get maxed out pretty quickly. Anglers stand on the dam, and campers loiter in the little gravel parking lot, despite the no camping signs. I once saw several truckloads of people pull up, get out, and wander up a hillside overlooking the lake to scatter the ashes of a loved one. When they came back down to their trucks, most of them left, but a few stayed to fish.

Anyway, the solitude was nice, an unexpected gift from the fishing gods: my own personal lake. A few swallows, or maybe swifts—I can't say which—circled and dove and kept me company.

You can fish this pond without a boat, but I set mine up anyway, finned into the middle and caught a grayling right away, somewhere between eight and ten inches.

I had forgotten about the grayling. All around me fish rose, a steady note that lasted the entire day. I looked closely at the water. No mayflies flew, no caddis fluttered. A few damsels flittered about, but most had gone AWOL. The water looked like a bug soup of old casings, bits of flotsam in various shapes and sizes. Something small and pale stood out in this mess, and I guessed the fish had keyed in on some kind of midge emerger. I couldn't quite make it out and doubted I had anything to match it anyway, so I tied on a small blue-winged olive pattern. It didn't look like much, just feathers on a size-20 hook, but it caught fish.

I picked up one Apache trout and five or six grayling that morning, took a break, dug around the truck for some lunch, but the best I could come up with was a peanut butter and M&M sandwich. On the way back to the water, I got tangled up in some old blue fishing line on the shore. Monofilament can get caught in the nests of eagles or ospreys and trap the chicks, so I gathered it all up, including the fly at the end of it, an elk hair caddis.

When the blue-wing stopped working, that elk hair caddis worked. When that stopped working, a peacock lady with a blue bead worked. The song "Tangled up in Blue" rolled around in my head as I tied it on, and an Apache trout took it. The next fish flipped off almost as quickly as he got on, but he flashed enough for me to see it was another Apache, and a good fish, maybe in the fourteen- to sixteen-inch range.

I switched back to dries. An osprey circled, crashed the water but came up empty. A little while later it circled back and plunged in again, and this time came up with a fish in its talons. It did a few laps over the lake while I missed a couple risers that bumped my fly. Showoff.

After a while I got off the water, gathered up my stuff, and took a drive through the Wallow Fire burn scar. The fire burned in 2011 after a couple of tourists walked away from their camp to go fishing. It burned more than half a million acres, surpassing Rodeo-Chediski as the largest wildfire in Arizona history. Entire hillsides remain bare to this day, save for a few green shrubs, the bones of old spruce and fir going back to ground.

The stream I had hoped to fish looked pretty low, so I kept going, the drive broken up by big views, a hen turkey that crossed the road with a few poults in tow. I made a mental note to come back in the spring, then drove back to my own personal lake.

And I caught fish. When it started to get late, I decided to head back to camp. A maze of elk and mule deer awaited on the roads, but I made it.

By then I had tired of chasing the calendar and decided to get ahead of the game, fish for smallmouth, head home. If you're struggling to catch trout in warm weather, maybe the solution isn't a cooler lake but a warm-water fish. So a couple of days later I broke camp and headed into the hills, far off the beaten path. The truck rumbled over a two-track path, a series of boulder fields, and each rock pile looked worse than the one before it, each axle bender more dicey than the last, the ruts deeper, the stakes higher. I wondered if had lost my mind. I parked about half a mile from the river, my stomach in knots, thinking about the drive out. I grabbed some gear and strung up a rod.

Smallmouth crashed my buggers and chased my blues away. I took dozens of fish that afternoon, and made a nice little camp back at the truck, no fire, while the stars circled overhead. The feeding frenzy continued the next morning, and the road didn't seem nearly as bad when I drove out in the midday sun. I came away feeling that I had taken charge, controlled my own destiny and all that, but it didn't last. It never does.

Summer passed in a series of hot days, the hottest on record in Phoenix, and in July, when I headed back to the mountains, my kick boat fell apart at the seams. After about twenty years of service, you could say it had a pretty good run, but a hole in the fabric around one of the pontoons started to give, and I heard popping sounds on the boat ramp as I topped it off with air. I took it back to camp, patched it with generous wraps of duct tape, and managed to take some healthy rainbows from it over the next couple of days, but I couldn't justify keeping the thing on the water much longer. I started boat shopping, and by autumn I had picked up a used kick boat and a new thirteen-foot raft.

We tell ourselves we let our fish go, but some of them stay with us for a lifetime. The promise of summer burns away, and we keep at it until that one day when we look back on all that has passed. The bend of the rod. The smallmouth in their fury. Sound of a kick boat coming apart at the seams. A drive down the Devil's Highway. Lake Solitude, where grayling and Apache trout rise all day long.

20. Back to the River

THE FISHING CAMP SAT on the banks of a river in Arizona, and the only person I knew there was lying in a box. His name was Chris. I hadn't seen him in years. We never actually had a falling out; we just drifted apart and stayed that way, the way people do when life rolls along at the pace of rivers: fast, slow, clear, roiling, rising, and falling through turns of weather or season. The kids wanted to scatter their father's ashes at his favorite fishing spot and invited several people out for the occasion. It was mid-May and getting warm, not a cloud in the sky. I showed up with a 6-weight rod and lots of flies with rubber legs, some camping gear, a bucket of memories.

About four decades ago, I followed Chris and a few other people from the Midwest to Arizona. We were young, college degrees hot off the presses, and thought we would live forever. I can picture him still, standing there with a big smile, blond hair, bronze skin from all those days in the sun. He's sitting at the bar. He's out there on the dance floor. He's cracking up at some stupid joke. He was cocksure and full of laughs, while I had questions, doubts, and not much of a plan, other than to find work and start a life in the West.

Office work bored Chris, so he took up carpentry. Not long after that he became a job boss on a construction site in Scottsdale, which is how I wound up working for him one summer. The fact that I had no carpentry experience didn't matter because every crew had a grunt—someone who carried boards, mixed mud, humped things from point A to point B.

We started at first light, so we could finish by the time it was good and hot. When the project began, a foreman grabbed a few sheets of plywood and some two-by-fours and built a shelter by the lumberyard, then added a workbench, table saw, a bunch of sawhorses, a few benches to sit on. A set of blueprints laid out the project page by page: a sprawling hotel with hundreds of arches, which we made there in the yard. Carpentry, I have to say, was a blast. I carried stuff, cut boards, hammered things, stapled the fleshy part of my hand to a piece of plywood. Our little patch of shade became a gathering place where people stopped by to shoot the breeze or drink beer at quitting time. We worked together, laughed together, a brotherhood of nails and sweat and beer in the desert. I rarely saw Chris. When we finished, the company would lay off most of us nailbenders, and we would scatter to the wind until the next job, and the one after that. But we didn't think too much about the future. We rose early, drove out to the edge of a growing metropolis, and we worked, the sun burning down, and we laughed and cursed, and swung our hammers all summer long.

Construction helped get me through the better part of a year, but eventually I landed a copy desk gig that allowed me to go to grad school by day, work at night, and fish on weekends, without the disruption of layoffs. By then I had the fishing bug and a sense that the move to Arizona might work out—the mild winters, big country, the bass fishing and high-country trout. In the summer, I left Phoenix for the cool mountain air every other weekend, exploring lakes and streams, hills and valleys. Then I learned about the Red and became obsessed. The Red starts out as a high-country trout stream that snakes through a labyrinth of mixed conifer, then drops into lower elevations where it becomes a smallmouth river. Deer, turkeys, and black bears wander the banks, which can grow tangled in willow, alder, and piles of driftwood. The volcanic rock pushes up in rough hills or cliffs that shoot up like skyscrapers and cut off passage, so you cross to the other bank for a time. The smallmouth feed on crawdads, hellgrammites, the odd damsel, hopper or caddis, and I fished with bait at first—usually crawdads out of the stream. The economy of showing up with nothing but a rod, reel, dip net, and bait bucket fascinated me. I switched to lures, then flies. The years rolled by.

I met Chris at the Red from time to time at camps perched above the river. He had become a father of three and had made new friends, including a guy named Bob, a real-deal fly fisherman who used a strike indicator and talked about places like the San Juan River, which sounded exotic and beyond my range, but would fall into the rotation soon enough. The last time I saw Bob, I had picked up a cheap fly rod, which I tried to learn how to cast on my own. He told me it would be impossible to teach myself how to fly-fish because at some point I would need a guide to show me the mends. But guides cost money, and so I muddled through the best I could with what I had.

I didn't see a lot of Chris then, he of the three-child household, and the details of what happened next remain sketchy. He had an affair, followed by a hasty divorce. Then he withdrew, and I let him, though I stayed in touch with his wife and consider her a dear friend. I had my own life to manage, my own marriage and divorce to deal with. I finally hired a guide and learned about those mends.

Fly-fishing opened up new worlds, and I went forth as if shot out of a cannon. The entire West lay before me, and I had hatches to follow, creeks to fish, lakes to float, mountains to climb. I spent soggy nights in wilderness camps, chased rumors of big browns, and fished small streams. I followed rivers, the lifeblood of the West, through canyons, burn scars, and meadows. San Juan River rainbows haunted my dreams. It comes back to me now in bits and pieces: thousands of fish, a few beers, campfires, brookies, cuts, natives. A life.

By the time I got word that Chris had died, we could all look into the rearview mirror of life and get an eyeful. Dave told me the story. How Chris lived alone at the time. How he fell and hit his head on something, nobody there to get help.

Not long after this I got word that the kids wanted to scatter Chris's ashes in the Red, and a couple of weeks later I got a text, then another that showed where they would be. I knew the place well. You could drive right down to the river, one of the few places that allowed such a luxury, though the last four hundred yards or so you barrel down a boulder-strewn rutted hillside—a real tire grabber. I left the house on a Friday night, camped in the desert, and finished the drive in the morning.

Most of our group was on the water when I arrived. I sat and shot the breeze with a guy named Eric for a while, then strung up a rod. Over the years I had fished this section several times and could conjure up all kinds of memories. Downstream: a few nice honey holes, camping on a beach, skinny-dipping, a couple of bears, hundreds of fish. Upstream remained less familiar, though Dennis and I, wearing heavy packs, headed that way once. Not far from the truck we found ourselves in a street fight on a tangled slope with thorny thickets, Spanish bayonet, prickly pear, and scree. When we got back down to the water, the fish bit like crazy. I can hear the creak of his reel, feel the tug of fish after fish on my 6-weight, the splash as they came to hand.

Eric showed me the route they took, which bypassed the stabby section that Dennis and I took a few years back. It had its share of ankle rollers, but we got to the river without breaking any bones. I got into my first smallmouth right away. Runoff comes early in Arizona, and the river had dropped to a clear steady flow, with just enough water for the fish to hold in. I headed upstream and caught a lot of fish before it was time to go back to camp.

I had seen Chris's kids growing up at various stages in life, but never spent much time with them, and was struck by how much they reminded me of their parents. The sound of her voice, the way his son took charge of camp, the gestures and mannerisms. We built a fire out of stout juniper logs and celebrated a life. The talk tended to stories of fish and fishing as cold beers came out, as daylight faded, as meat sizzled over hot coals, as music played, and laughter rippled into the trees, a hint of cedar in the air, the stars bright.

In the morning we packed our stuff and gathered at the river. Until then it had been like any other fishing camp, a bunch of nail-benders, a nurse, various roughnecks and dabblers—tough, strapping backcountry anglers, but then everyone got misty-eyed. Voices broke and memories swirled like a hurricane. The kids talked about how much Chris enjoyed the Red, and his daughter said we had all played a part in his life. It had been so long since I had seen him, and I wondered how that could be true. But then I remembered I was the one who introduced Chris to the Red. Well.

He's stopping by the lumberyard. He's giving me a hard time about something. He's laughing his ass off. He's standing in the river, casting a lure into a shady nook on the far bank.

I wish Bob, the fly-fisher at those old camps, could have been there, but he's gone. Others have gone as well, a growing list of folks who have died too young. I'm not sure what I thought was going to happen, back in those days when we were young and the world was full of possibilities, but it wasn't this.

The sun shined, and we gathered at the river, the beautiful, beautiful river, where they poured his ashes into a riffle. A white stripe of ash ran along the stream bottom, which summer rains would blow out in a couple of months. Memories followed us as we walked away and started the long drive back to town. It had been a good couple of days. The weather was nice, and everyone caught fish. Chris would have liked that.

Part III
Dystopia

21. Yellow Trout

EMERSON WAITS. A MIST rises off Christmas Tree Lake on the White Mountain Apache Reservation, and trout nose along the weed line as we cast. "Closer," he says. Sunlight struggles behind a cloudbank and a hen turkey calls from tall and distant trees. Not long after this, a dozen turkeys come down to feed along the shoreline. A muskrat swims by, a heron flies overhead, fish rise, and I manage to land one, lost in a daydream when it strikes, a golden flash. He makes a few runs before I net him, remove the hook, feel the soft belly on the release. We're fishing for Apache trout, a native to Arizona, and Emerson catches several before things slow to a crawl. I am waiting, he is waiting, and the morning unfolds slowly—the clouds lifting, the fish rising, the sound of fly lines lifting off the water.

Emerson Craig grew up on the Navajo Nation. One day he came across an old woman at a lake, catching fish, so he had to ask. "What are you using?"

"A bug."

"A bug?"

She had a spinning rod but was using what anglers call a bubble to get the fly out on the water. He learned to fish with a bug and a bubble, got older, took up a fly-fishing, married an Apache woman. He occasionally guides and is well known in the Arizona fly-fishing community. When I call to ask about native trout, he invites me up to check out the bite at Christmas Tree.

Apache trout have a golden hue, with black spots, olive, a splash of yellow along the jaw, as if shards of sunlight, or aspen leaves, have fallen into the water and embedded themselves in the local fish. The story of Apache trout roughly follows the same plotline as that of other native trout species across the West—the fish nearly done in by mining, overgrazing, dams, roads, irrigation, overfishing, hybridization, and hungry brown trout. By the early twentieth century, they lived in remote headwaters of Fort Apache in eastern Arizona. Around 1940, though, the White Mountain Apache Tribal Council outlawed fishing in some of those streams. In 2024, the US Fish and Wildlife Service removed the Apache trout from the endangered species list.

For years, nobody knew much about the Apache trout. Biologists thought the White Mountain fish were Gila trout, another native fish that faced extinction. So the tribe offered its protection and closed the streams, some of which remain off-limits to this day.

In 1965, the tribe cut a seventy-foot blue spruce tree near Sun and Moon Creeks, held a ceremony, and shipped it to Washington, DC. The tree was decorated with thousands of colored bulbs and put up near the White House for the holidays during the Johnson administration. The president plugged in the lights on a mid-December day and delivered a Christmas greeting, with an Apache delegation in attendance.

The tribe had already decided to dam the confluence of the creeks when it cut the tree. When the lake filled, they named it Christmas Tree and stocked it with native fish from Ord, Firebox, and Deep Creeks. In 1969, the tribe received an award from the Department of Interior for its work in conservation.

The council had closed more streams to fishing by 1972 when Robert Rush Miller identified the Apache trout as a unique species. Miller was the student, colleague, and son-in-law of Carl Leavitt

Hubbs, a prominent ichthyologist. They rambled the West over rutted roads that jarred batteries loose and poked holes in gas tanks, which they plugged with chewing gum, the running boards of their cars piled high with so much gear that they had to lash the driver's side door shut. Miller had already identified the Gila trout as a unique species, and he began to suspect that the White Mountain trout were biologically different. When he described the fish in an academic journal, he wrote that the tribe had saved it from extinction and named it *Salmo apache*, Apache trout.

By this time, the Arizona Game and Fish Department and US Fish and Wildlife Service had started to survey Arizona streams as part of a nationwide inventory of America's wildlife. The nation had begun to examine the impacts of modern life on the natural world and rethink its approach to land management and wildlife conservation. Aldo Leopold had written about watching a Mexican wolf die, the green fire in her eyes fading. Whooping crane numbers had dropped to a handful, California condor numbers had dipped to about sixty, the jaguar had been pushed out of the United States. Smog clouded the Los Angeles skyline, and rivers caught fire.

When Congress passed the Endangered Species Act of 1973 (ESA), its vote was nearly unanimous. The act faced a major test when it ran up against a dam on the Little Tennessee River. Locals who lived along the river, mostly farmers and anglers, pointed out that the government had already dammed just about every inch of the Little Tennessee. They saw the dam for what it was—pork-barrel politics, a waste of time and money. When researchers found that a fish called the snail darter lived in the river, a fish found nowhere else in the world at that time, the locals said the dam would harm the fish, so they put the ESA to the test and took their case all the way to the Supreme Court. The court, in a 6–3 ruling, said that while it seemed curious that a three-inch fish could block the multimillion-dollar Tellico Dam project, the law's intent was clear.

"The Supreme Court said all species that are at risk of extinction, shall be protected at any cost. Whatever the cost is, we will protect them," said Lowell Baier, an attorney who has written extensively about the act.

Baier said the ruling made sense because ecosystems rely on small animals, plants, and bugs to function properly. But Congress operated on a system of pork that persists to this day. Some Congressmen had a tough time selling the act to voters, who questioned the value of snail darters and other small animals, and the bipartisan spirit didn't last. Lawmakers started to backpedal and withdraw their support for the act. They told constituents they thought they had voted to protect animals like the grizzly, the eagle, and the bison, species known as charismatic megafauna. Baier said he has read all of the testimony and sat in on some hearings while Congress discussed the legislation.

"And Congress was very thorough, in looking at the evidence before them. They knew, perfectly well, that this stood for all species, all species regardless of size. And so it was an easy copout for them to say, oh gee whiz, we thought it was only for megafauna."

At the time, dams fueled the machinery of Congress, which reacted to the Supreme Court ruling by amending the law just five years after it had passed. And so it created a committee that could oversee the law's application and decide, in effect, if a species would live or die—the God Squad. The committee thought the dam was a bad idea, too, not because of the snail darter, but on economic grounds. It ruled against the project in a unanimous vote.

The project moved forward. Congress did not care about endangered species or the farmers forced from their homes or free-flowing rivers or a two-inch fish or a three-inch fish or hydroelectric power or flood control. It cared about politics, horse trading, and the flow of money.

Lawmakers who favored the project portrayed their opponents—these farmers and anglers who gathered at potlucks and sold T-shirts to raise money—as environmental extremists. The label stuck. Local newspaper editors, who knew better but could not be bothered to do their jobs, did not encourage their reporters to write about the project, and the national media rarely dug any deeper.

When nobody was looking, a couple of Congressmen slipped a provision that exempted Tellico Dam from the ESA. Federal marshals evicted the last families living along the river, and the snail darter took the blame for delaying a project that never should have left the drawing board. The snail darter did not go extinct—biologists found another population nearby, but the case received a lot of publicity, if not scrutiny, and the story persists—"tiny fish halts progress."

Congress had found a way to neutralize the ESA. Wave the banner of economic growth. Label your opponents radical environmentalists. Move forward.

The ESA has helped save hundreds of species from going extinct, but it is widely misunderstood and raises a lot of questions about costs, tradeoffs, biodiversity, genetics, and our culture. Hundreds of thousands of projects have "triggered consultations, but studies have found that more than 95 percent are resolved informally and virtually none stop[s] a project in its tracks," Mitch Tobin writes in *Endangered: Biodiversity on the Brink*. When it comes to conflicts between people and animals, people win.

We can take each project, break it down, weigh costs against benefits, listen attentively as each party tells its story, analyze the comments on the back pages of thick reports, await the judge's ruling on each court case that comes down the pike, tell ourselves that we have been thoughtful, reasonable, sober, and attentive to the needs of our fellow creatures.

Dig through the entrails of the law, however, and you will find a world in which public input gets pushed aside, in which government agencies skirt the law and ignore whistleblowers, in which lawmakers slip riders into bills in the dead of night, in which no law can stop that thing we call progress. That is, once all is said and done, everything remains business as usual. You will find lawyers, guns, and money—just like the song. The complexities of each moment break down when you step back and look at the body of work. Every project moves forward and everything gets built.

See the mine, the subdivision, the mall, the border wall, the solar array, the cattle on the range, the wind farm, the dam, the telescope, the interstate, the bright eyes of a wolf as she draws her last breath. People win, money keeps moving, and the undertow of apathy remains strong.

This does not mean that the act has failed. Nor should it diminish the good work that biologists, researchers, nonprofits, and government agencies have done. Engineers redraw projects, researchers find new pockets of habitat, lawsuits help root out government sloth and malfeasance, fish barriers go up, birds hatch, radio collars track beasts as they move in the dark. Some species have rebounded—you can find any number of success stories, the Apache trout among them. But news about endangered animals gets lost in the everyday sound and fury, and the general public just doesn't hear much about these issues. You also get the sense that a lot of people in our society would choose freeways, dams, and subdivisions over fish or birds. You can find anglers in Arizona who remain indifferent to the Apache trout's fate because they say the fish lack heart, size, or intelligence.

Fish and Wildlife delisted the Apache trout in 2024, but we will care for these fish in perpetuity. Fish barriers will need maintenance, and the state must guard against rogue brown trout, rainbows, budget cuts, bucket biologists, apathy, catastrophic fire, and floodwaters. This is the new world, in which mankind manages the birds and the beasts, the fish, the ebb and flow of field and stream, things that once worked so well on their own.

The scene plays out in my mind over and over: an autumn day, fishing for yellow trout on a small lake in the Arizona hills, where a bald eagle rides the thermals. Endangered species coming back from the edge, in the sky above and the water before me. Later, big caddisflies come off and I catch fish on dry flies until a storm blows through and knocks the bugs off the water. The moon rises, and elk bugle in the night. The evening air has a bite and I make camp, build a fire, and stare into the red core. I can feel them strike, picture the fish held briefly in sunlight, the yellow jaw, tail splashing on release.

These images comfort me, as they should. But sooner or later, it's back to work, and new images will take their place: the cover page of a lawsuit in which plaintiffs state their complaints, a new report that models a warmer future, a thick tome on the various ways to look at wilderness or wildness or the vanishing beasts, words that remind us that pristine ground no longer exists, that a bleak future may lie ahead. I grind through each day, the hours pass, and the clatter of keyboards sets my teeth on edge.

And so I go back to rivers. To high-country lakes and skinny creeks. Days on the water at first and last light. Emerson's waiting and rings on the water. *Closer*. Caddis flutter, dark clouds move over the mountains. A cold stream winds through yellow asters and green grass. Hazy summer morning, clumps of elk fur, antler, and bone. We can't go back. Saving the Apache trout, or the bison, or some exotic bird won't transport us back to the past, to some backcountry Eden, to some idyllic state of nature. But it might help fulfill our moral obligation to save something for future generations. The sun comes up, the clouds fade away, and fish rise in the shallows.

22. Gila Trout

SUMMER PASSED IN A blink. It started with full lakes and high-running streams, and each day went by in flashes of color: golden browns, bronze slabs of river smallmouth, the silver and red of fat rainbows. By autumn I was obsessed with native trout and the color was yellow.

The trout held exactly where you would expect them to—in seams along cut banks, in plunge pools, and in deep holes. September. Asters withered on the sunlit meadow. Storm clouds swirled and thunder crashed in the peaks, the aspens aflutter. Mosquitoes rose up out of alpine bogs and seeps and launched a furious attack as I made my way to the stream, where Apache trout rose to dry flies.

I fished until I had squandered the better part of an afternoon, then headed back to the truck, drove awhile, and looked for a place to camp. The next day I headed to New Mexico to fish for Gila trout, and these, too, crashed dry flies as I walked upstream.

It's tempting to say that catching native trout is a purist endeavor, but most of us have come too far and know too much—restoring native fish populations is time-consuming, difficult, and expensive. Our ideas about native fish can get tangled in history and science, in thorny philosophical questions about nature, culture, angling and politics.

When the summer began I was just an average fun hog. Then Cinda told me about Gila trout in New Mexico. About a week later I woke before dawn, fumbled around camp in the dark, and drove out to meet her.

When we got to the stream, a canyon wren sang in the trees and the notes fell one by one, as if fluttering out of the cliffs, or falling from the branches of a towering sycamore. We walked about a quarter mile, dropped into a little slot canyon, where Cinda flipped dry flies into tight windows for most of the morning, and the fish grabbed them with abandon. The stream tumbled all around us through remnants of ancient volcanic squall, around boulder-choked passages, and into a narrow slot, until the canyon opened and the water broke on shallow cobble.

I didn't have a New Mexico fishing license. We made a few attempts to get me one, but the sleepy little pit stops in rural New Mexico didn't give us many options. One place was closed, if memory serves. Then we tried getting one at a gas station with a shaky internet connection that stalled out a few times before we gave up and decided to move on. So I followed with my camera, watching and enjoying the day.

By midmorning she had caught several fish and we pushed on to another stream, where things slowed down for a while as she worked a stretch of shallow pocket water. We passed abandoned mining flotsam, blackberry bramble, and bear scat, working our way upstream until we had walked a mile and fish started to bite. A few weeks later, armed with a fishing license and a 4-weight, I caught dozens of these yellow trout on my own.

State and federal biologists have used a variety of tools to restore Gila trout—pack mules, helicopters, genetic research, a state-of-the-art hatchery, DNA detection technology, micro-chipped trout, and shoe leather, but the Gila trout itself may be the best tool at their disposal. It took decades for biologists to figure these fish out. The rest of us have a lot to learn. Gila trout are beautiful, resilient, and a pleasure to fish for. They have evolved to withstand extreme drought and warm water, brutal conditions for browns and rainbows, but they don't always get a fair shake.

The Gila trout's ancestors arrived sometime during the Pleistocene and were locked into the watershed when glacial epochs shaped the New Mexico landscape about 25,000–50,000 years ago. They lived here when aboriginal people known as the Mogollon built cliff dwellings in the hills, when Spanish soldiers marched up from the south, when American trappers came through in search of beaver pelts, when prospectors dug for gold, and soldiers chased Geronimo. They lived here before the first cowboy rode, before the first saloon or cathouse opened its doors. Early settlers reported catching about fish a minute, with an average of about twelve inches. But after a couple of decades of overfishing, the trout were in trouble. By 1923, Game and Fish was trying to raise Gila trout in a hatchery. It didn't go well.

By this time, government fishheads had begun a love affair with rainbow trout. Over the years, biologists learned that the rainbow can be "anything we want it to be," said Nathan Wiese, a fisheries biologist with the US Fish and Wildlife Service. Anders Halverson documents this story in *An Entirely Synthetic Fish*.

Rainbow trout adapt well to hatchery life. You can breed them to spawn early and grow faster. They resist disease, have a high tolerance for crowding and handling. They can live on a diet of pellets, though you might have to teach them to eat bugs before releasing them. You can raise them quickly, haul them in an airplane or the back of a truck. Across the West, when native fish populations dropped, biologists frequently replaced them with hatchery fish. The rainbow trout became a product, a deliverable with synthetic genes, engineered and mass-produced for an unquestioning public. A rubber fish.

Rainbow trout don't just take over the stream—they take over the gene pool. They spawn in the springtime, when native Gila, Apache, and cutthroat trout spawn. In 1966, biologists who surveyed New Mexico's streams found a lot of hybrids. They listed the Gila trout as endangered.

Fishheads historically assumed, as did the rest of us, that putting more fish in the water today meant more fish in the long run, but it doesn't necessarily work that way. In the mid-1960s, Montana biologist Dick Vincent found that dumping a bunch of hatchery fish into a stream can have consequences, not all of them good. Wild fish have a pecking order and don't waste much energy fighting for position, which can expose them to predators. Hatchery fish lack etiquette and judgment. They carry on like barbarians in the buffet line, pushing and shoving and checking out the ladies. When Vincent produced data that showed adding hatchery trout might mean *fewer* fish in the long run, the state abandoned its stocking program for one that favored wild trout. Today Montana has some of the best trout fishing in the world.

Halverson's work is interesting and informative, a road map of policy and history, but it's not clear how that history might guide us. Every stream is different, and what works in Montana might not work the same way in arid Arizona or New Mexico. Anglers have a difficult time imagining the West without browns. Brown trout—aggressive, fall spawning, adaptable, and resilient—elbow aside natives and can establish wild populations if left alone. They do well on a lot of remote streams, so anglers remain suspicious of any program to replace them with native fish. Various constituencies of anglers have emerged over the years: the rainbow clan, the brown trout clan, the wild trout clan, fly-fishers, bait soakers, tourists. Many have fierce opinions, and a favorite stream.

While biologists managed trout, foresters tried to manage timber. For decades, foresters discussed the purpose of fire in the woods. Some said it played a natural role and that light burning would keep a forest healthy and natural. Professional foresters dismissed the practice, and said that "Paiute Forestry" had no place in modern resource management, which valued timber above all. The Forest Service chose to suppress fire in all its forms.

Mines played out, people moved on, boomtowns fell on hard times and became ghost towns, the forest grew thicker, tourists kept coming, the Gila trout retreated to higher elevations.

As fishery biologists tried to untangle the genetics of trout, the Forest Service realized something might be said for that Piute Forestry thing and talked of managing forests with light burning. Figuring out how and where to burn, with a century of fuel on the ground and towns firmly established in and around the forests, was not easy, and so the agency dithered on the details. In the late 1980s, fire started doing the job itself.

In the Southwest, the rainy season follows fire season. Trees and brush slow down runoff, but a fire-scarred hill can become a waterslide, shooting mud and ash into trout streams, cutting off oxygen, killing fish. A big wildfire can erase years of native fish recovery in New Mexico, but biologists have learned to adjust. When a wildfire strikes, they pull fish before the monsoon comes and place them in hatcheries. They feed them crickets, mealworms, and maggots laced with commercial fish food for about six months. This allows the fish to transition from the wild to an artificial diet.

Biologists have also found a silver lining to some of these fires. After floods scour a stream and nearly wipe it clean of all fish, they can restock that stream with natives. They have the technology to take a genetic fingerprint of a stream to see whether any fish remain, to microchip a trout, scan it later, and see where its ancestors lived.

At Mora National Fish Hatchery they don't raise natives in traditional concrete raceways. They use circular tanks with a simulated current.

"It's kind of a misnomer to call it a raceway. There's no racing at all. It's just a pool. It's a lazy river," Wiese said. Grad students who study flow rates have found that simulating current creates a stronger, more resilient fish.

"What we've found is if you swim that fish at two body lengths a second, they're a whole different fish. We're building muscle. We're putting them on a treadmill." They add shade and rocks to simulate wild conditions. The trout come out stronger than the average hatchery fish, ready to go after whatever floats downstream.

Like their cousins, the Apache trout, Gila trout have a reputation for being small. Wiese points out that a series of actions have pushed natives into skinny headwaters, the shallowest water in their range, where food is scarce, the growing season short, the holes small. I can think of a lot of skinny brown trout streams that fit that description. Put small fish in a small stream and they'll stay that way for the most part.

The undertow of history has shaped Southwestern trout populations, along with science, politics, ecology, drought, state policy, federal oversight, wildfire, angler angst, human appetites, climate change. The resilience of trout. We have put-and-take lakes and streams, wild fish, natives, rainbows, browns, cutthroats, brookies, and various hybrids, the biology tangled in knots. Depending on your outlook, it's either a glorious buffet or a hell of a mess. I suspect most anglers don't care as long as the fish bite. Which makes you wonder why so many of us love to fish for brown trout. Many words describe browns—tough, scrappy, challenging, but also brooding and tight-lipped.

The dozens of yellow trout that took my flies that summer and fall got my attention, along with a paragraph in the Gila Trout Recovery Plan that said early settlers in New Mexico caught a fish a minute. It's a throwaway sentence in a government report that soon gets down to the brass tacks of peer-reviewed data on stream hydrology and invertebrates, but it stands out. Maybe native fish restoration isn't such a fool's errand after all.

By November, the trees had shed most of their leaves and the bite had slowed. Cinda and I pulled on waders, caught a few fish, drove up bone-jarring gravel to a ghost town in the pines, and wandered backroads to scout some new water. We came back down the mountain in the near dark as a pale yellow moon cleared the treetops. The trout, well, they're still out there, in ancient volcanic folds of western New Mexico, under broken down mining timbers on cliffs and banks, among the ghosts of various legends that haunt these canyons. Come springtime the fish will rise—and in the summer and fall, too. They'll rush past your dropper to take your dry. They'll fin away with a splash on the release.

You can only catch an Apache trout or a Gila trout in one place: the rough hills of Arizona and New Mexico. Native trout remain as vital to the Southwest as the Grand Canyon, as saguaro cactus, as yucca blooms and roadrunners and Geronimo's ghost, as high desert hills that rise up to mountainous spreads of ponderosa and bramble, bear, elk, and trout streams. The moon rises over dark ribbons of asphalt that wind through the hills, into horizons that roll out like waves, and we drive.

23. Fire on the Mountain

I MUST BE LOSING my mind. My dreams have grown dark, and the trees keep trying to tell me something. They grabbed my attention a few years ago in southern Colorado, and I've thought about them ever since. The days had passed in sunlight, the song of mountain water, green grass and golden browns, the spots of brookies. One afternoon I settled into camp and saw a band of spruce and fir in the distance, dead trees that had dropped their needles, their hue a grayish brown or brownish gray, not so much a color as an absence of color, a gray pallor of death. They had been there all along, but for some reason they stood out that afternoon. A few days later I broke camp and hiked out, footsore and weary, drove over the pass into the next valley, and the next, past one gray hill after another.

Researchers say that several species of bark beetles have come to feed in our forests because climate change has set the table. A few decades ago the trees would have released toxins in their sap to block these invaders, or the bugs would die off in the winter. But drought has robbed the trees of the moisture that helps produce enough sap, and winters have grown mild. The forests are also overgrown, so the bugs spread quickly.

Bark beetles evolved with pine trees, but things have changed, and the extent of their damage continues to grow. As anglers, we should snap to attention when we see a forest without color or wildfire scars or bathtub rings on reservoirs, but for the most part, we don't. We visit the forest on weekends, along with hikers and other tourists, and turn things back to foresters on weekdays. I'm not sure we have that luxury any more.

The beetles range across the West, and the trees they kill prime the forest to burn in apocalyptic swells that ravage watersheds and kill fish. Historically, small fires burned and cleared the forest floor on a regular basis, but big fires have come after more than a century of managing the forest for profit, which is to say, putting out fires. Early American foresters considered fire a waste of timber and baked firefighting into their DNA, which resulted in a fuel buildup on the forest floor that has led to the magnitude and frequency of the blazes we see today. The forests recover—usually—because nature has a way of filling a void with its capacity for replanting slopes with oak or aspen or walnut. But these fires can leave deep scars, recovery takes time, and more fires will come.

Although we think of forests as places where nature calls the shots, government agencies frequently try to manage them: the animals culled, the rivers harnessed and inventoried to the last drop, the grass grazed, the trees cultivated like crops—to this day the Forest Service has its home within the Department of Agriculture. After more than a century of bookkeeping, we can see profit and loss, shrinking inventory, the balance sheets in various stages of disarray. Botanists, biologists, and other researchers count the dead, assess the damage, survey the literature, and work the hatcheries. Their reports are grim, and even a cursory look at them can make you weep.

Three of America's twenty-eight species and subspecies of trout have gone extinct, and, according to one study, many are down to under 25 percent of their historic range. The numbers reflect a legacy of industrial pollution, ag runoff, grazing, diversion, and roads. Dams, in turn, have fragmented streams and choked off migration corridors.

The fossil record tells us that Salmonidae swam in lakes and streams when dinosaurs walked the earth as Robert J. Behnke writes in *Trout and Salmon of North America*. An ancestor of trout, known as *Eosalmo driftwoodensis*, lived in North America about fifty million years ago, as plates shifted, as ice sheets moved, and as the Rockies reached for the sky. The fractured land isolated trout populations and gave us cutthroats, steelhead, rainbows, Yaqui trout, Gila trout—fish that range from Canada to Mexico. They were here when humans crossed over the Bering Strait, while ancient Rome burned, when the redwoods you see today first took root, when General George Crook fished for cuts, and Custer fell at the Battle of Little Bighorn.

They took the bait when the first settlers dropped their lines in the water. Grainy black-and-white photos confirm that these newcomers had an appetite for trout. As catch-and-release anglers, we cringe when we see these snapshots, a few dozen fish strung up, the two or three proud anglers that flank either side of the frame. History tells us native fish vanished from one drainage after another as government agencies built roads and dams, cattle devoured grass, mines and smelters fouled streams, foresters put out fires, and fuel loads built up over the course of a century. The list goes on.

Foresters have since learned that ponderosa forests in particular evolved with fires, and removing them from the landscape has had consequences. Biologists have learned more about native fish and the threats they face. About the time scientists began to get up to speed in wood and stream, to document the consequences of industry on our watersheds, the planet warmed and everything changed.

Climate change has reduced snowpack, warmed lakes and creeks, and disrupted stream flows. Rising temperatures drive trout to higher elevations. Organisms that threaten trout, salmon, and their food supply now feast in these warm waters, and so we add words such as rock snot and megafire to our vocabulary.

Throughout the West, fishery biologists must balance the needs of trout with those of ranchers, utilities, and government agencies such as the Bureau of Reclamation and the Forest Service. They are also up against the Mining Law of 1872, miles of red tape, lobbyists, the Koch brothers, oligarchs, and interest groups that want to use public lands for profit. Because society needs copper and roads and hydroelectric power, the projects that threaten trout habitat seem necessary, something that any *reasonable* person can get behind. The dire warnings of environmental groups may sound overwrought because, after all, the sun rises each day and life goes on. Their dystopian, apocalyptic worldview is a real buzzkill and offends a broad spectrum of interests: our urban lifestyle, our Midwestern values, the wealthy, the bourgeoisie, the working stiff trying to feed his family. And so people go back to work and leave politics to the politicians, who take money from industry lobbyists and get re-elected to maintain the status quo. Biologists stock fish to keep anglers happy, distracted, and silent. Apathy joins the beetle and the budworm at the table.

Some scientists say the climate crisis has become intertwined with a human-caused mass extinction, the sixth in the earth's history. Yet the average person struggles to get worked up about climate change. A few degrees warmer doesn't seem like all that much, and rising ocean levels don't seem all that dire to those who live inland. Warmer winters might seem rather pleasant to freezing Midwesterners, and few of us have ever seen a polar bear in the wild. The prospect of a warming planet remains abstract, math-intensive, a vision of some distant future, and the idea of mass extinction has yet to trickle down to the public at large.

But anglers can see the effects of a warming planet in lake and stream, in field and forest, a growing list of maladies that tells us the future has arrived: falling stream levels, warmer temperatures, hellfire in our forests, crashing salmon populations, the trout in a funk by mid-June. These reports do not describe some abstract concept, or something that *might* happen, or something that could happen in a few generations: It's happening now. In 2007, the Firehole River in Yellowstone National Park got so warm that fish died. Biologists must now toss summer fishing closures into their toolbox. One report says the United States could lose half of its trout habitat in a few decades.

Fly-fishers have every reason to take pride in their work on conservation, but not all of us have embraced this work, and some even remain skeptical of native fish restoration. Anglers love what they know, and tribal allegiances run deep. Armchair biologists complain that native trout don't fight as hard as brown trout, as if comparing chocolate to vanilla, but we may not have that luxury any more. We can't pat ourselves on the back for being conservationists, anglers who would rather starve than eat a trout, to quote Gierach, and then shrug or roll our eyes when we hear words such as climate change, extinction, native trout, or recovery.

There's no going back to the nineteenth century, but we can do better. We should enjoy the water and cling to what's left of our optimism. But it's no longer enough to be apolitical or apathetic, a climate change denier on Tuesdays and a catch-and-release angler on Saturdays. We need to look beyond our self-interest and stop thinking of streams as trout delivery systems.

The traditional model of saving one thing—the bison, the eagle, the condor, the cutthroat trout—has produced a few success stories, but history, science, philosophy, and common sense point to a new direction: Save habitat, nurture the system, not just one piece of it. So far the idea of a sixth extinction, wrapped in the complexities of a warming planet, remains obscure to the general public. Climate change has swallowed environmentalism, in part because people can see it happening, in part because the solution—building a new grid—remains simple and includes a long list of winners: new industries, new jobs, and electricity to people, tribes, and nations who have done without. The story of extinction carries a darker, more complex message, but it's getting harder to look away.

Fishing remains, at its core, a pastime for daydreamers and optimists, people who drive hundreds of miles to stand in the rain and cast in hopes that a fish will bite. Sometimes it's just a fool's hope, but it keeps us anchored, brings us closer to what's good in this world, and what's worth fighting for. Polls show that an overwhelming majority of westerners support conservation and the continued existence of public lands—things most of us can agree on without the usual political bile rising to the surface. Success comes in dribs and drabs, but it shows what's possible.

Montana's switch to wild fish once ruffled a lot of feathers, but the state now has some of the best trout fishing in the world. In the Northwest, biologists have begun to restore salmon runs, and dams that once seemed so necessary have come down. Natives recover. Streams rise from the dead. The planet rearranges itself, and trout find their way.

Or maybe I'm losing my mind. As I said, the trees keep trying to tell me something, and when I follow their string, it leads to this postapocalyptic, dystopian wood, dark dreams in broad daylight, backroom deals, dark money, and fire on the mountain. Clouds gather, rain pours, and I nap inside the tent. When the clouds part and the sun shines, I go fishing. A breeze stirs, and the river sings its song.

24. No Trespassing

NOTHING STEALS YOUR SOUL like a No Trespassing sign. You drive along a stretch of nice water, then start to look for a place to pull off when you see it: red on black, white on red, big and bold in all caps. You go bird hunting and see some good ground up ahead, but when you get closer you spot the fence, the sign, your world smaller and somewhat diminished. You see them in the Rockies, on barbed wire strung across a stream, on fence posts and tree trunks, so many that one day you mutter that the No Trespassing sign is the state flower of Colorado. New Mexico rolls out on a ribbon of asphalt and well-kept fence lines posted down to the square foot; farms, ranches and lodges, vacation homes, the massive land grants handed down by Spanish lords. Posted. No Trespassing. Private Property.

Public lands are the backbone of the American West. They account for about seventy percent of native trout water, and they are under attack. Sagebrush Rebels, state legislators, and political action committees want to do away with federal oversight, while robber barons buy vacation homes, put up gates, and seize their own personal trout streams. When the locals protest, they lawyer up. The conflict drags on for years.

Americans have looked west ever since the original colonies began to fill and settlers streamed over the Appalachian Mountains into the Ohio Valley. Beyond the Mississippi River, miles of unsettled ground stretched into the horizon, new frontiers claimed by the Spanish, the British, the French, all of it up for grabs, Stephen Ambrose writes. For nearly three centuries, European nations planted flags, built forts, drew up maps, and held land they settled sparsely or not at all. Spain struggled to hold all the lands it claimed to own and eventually lost its grip when Mexico declared its independence. Mexico, in turn, struggled for control over unruly tribes and belligerent Texans, its northern states boiling with unrest.

In those days, nothing moved faster than a horse—troops, supplies, communication. To claim ground was one thing, to possess it was another, and few could conceive how one nation could rule an entire continent. But Thomas Jefferson wondered whether America might stretch from coast-to-coast one day.

"More than any other man, he helped make that happen," Ambrose writes. Jefferson set events in motion with the Louisiana Purchase, a sweep of land from the Mississippi to the Rocky Mountains; no roads, no rails, bad maps, lots of indigenous folk who disputed our title.

Congress understood that settling these new lands was important. It pictured a nation of yeoman farmers and offered up new homesteads for a couple bucks an acre, then $1.25. By 1862, the government started to give it away. It gave land to railroad companies to spur investment—every other section on both sides of the tracks—until rails linked the nation. Federal troops and supplies moved swiftly in this new world, but still the government had too much land. Congress also gave land to the states, so they could sell it to raise money for schools. These gifts helped create the checkerboard patterns you see on maps to this day. The government continued to give land to homesteaders and allowed prospectors to dig where they pleased; eastern capital backed these ventures, and mining towns sprang up like mushrooms. For decades, Americans pushed west, driven by talk of cheap dirt, California gold, land where rain follows the plow. Mexico watched as its northern territories filled with warlords and American border crossers. The Sioux, the Comanche, and the Apache watched as settlers streamed in until the ground seethed with conflict and blood spilled across the plains.

As new territories formed, they found life difficult in these lands. They needed more people, more eastern capital, and generous helpings of federal aid. One by one, each territory applied for statehood, made promises, signed legally binding agreements in exchange for federal dollars and legal recognition. Each territory turned its unclaimed lands over to the feds, just as the original thirteen colonies had done when they became states.

The nation of yeoman farmers never materialized. The West had too much ground, not enough water, angry tribes, bad dirt. Farmers went broke and ranchers struggled. Land speculators found ways to snatch new ground in spite of laws written to discourage them. Even after Congress increased the size of a homestead to 640 acres in Western states, ranchers fattened their herds on nearby lands that had not been claimed. When the grass took a beating, they pushed onto tribal lands, their neighbor's turf. The West was big and lonely, its possibilities clouded by range wars, court battles, cattle heists, long winters, a drought so bad that cows died where they stood. Congress eventually passed the Taylor Grazing Act to protect grasslands and bring order to chaos, but critics say it changed little. The herdsmen came to think of themselves as tough and self-sufficient, but this was a myth, a story they told themselves and anyone who would listen. The truth was they had developed a complicated relationship with Washington.

Congress spent millions to make life easier for Westerners with dams, roads, and other improvements. The feds killed predators, put out forest fires at taxpayer expense, and kept grazing fees low. Ranchers got so used to their federal allotments of cheap grass, Bernard DeVoto writes, they "convinced themselves that it belonged to them."

But the land also belonged to the American taxpayer, who paid for it with blood and treasure. Trains and automobiles made visiting these distant states a favorite American pastime. The West was gritty and far-flung, an outdoor museum where the price of admission was a little gas money. For all its rough edges, it had outposts of civilization, national parks, Harvey Girls, dude ranches, the roadside attractions of Route 66, good fishing. The West was beautiful and bleak, with hundreds of thousands of acres that Congress couldn't give away. In 1976, Congress passed the Federal Land Policy Management Act, and the Great American Land Dump came to an end.

Sagebrush Rebels almost immediately began to rewrite this history and complain about federal lockups, grazing fees, and other injustices. The movement never really gained traction with a wider audience, in part because it was rooted in anarchy, and anarchists are bad at organizing. It also lacked solid legal footing, much less a coherent message. But it has never entirely gone away.

"They're like locusts," said Corey Fisher of Trout Unlimited. "Every decade or so they come back."

The movement has many layers, Jonathan Thompson observes, with spokesmen emerging on various levels—local upstarts, county commissioners, state legislators, US Senators posturing for the salt-of-the-earth bloc. Occasionally, the talk turns violent. In 2014, Cliven Bundy, the Nevada rancher who has racked up more than a million dollars in grazing fees, emerged as a mouthpiece for these saber rattlers, though he was not the first. This is the dark heart of the movement, which has led to standoffs in Nevada and Oregon.

But the movement has a backroom wing as well, where politicians pass bills, raise money, crank out misinformation, form committees, and explore legal options. In 2012, Utah passed a law demanding that Congress transfer title of its federal lands to the state. (Other states have proposed similar measures, which have either failed to pass or were vetoed.) National parks, wilderness, and Indian reservations would be exempt from this transfer. The rest would be reviewed by the Utah Public Lands Commission and possibly put up for sale. Nobody knows what will happen next, but it's easy to guess with some degree of accuracy. Some will likely go to oil and gas companies, some will go to timber companies, or mining companies, which will be free to operate with less oversight than they have now. Billionaire oligarchs will secure massive estates. Developers will snap up the rest. Smart money says that before long the gates will go up, the locks snapped shut, yet these yarn spinners say that state ownership will *improve* public access.

They have the support of various county governments and Americans for Prosperity, a group backed by the Koch brothers. Other groups pushing similar tales include the American Lands Council, the Pacific Legal Foundation, the American Legislative Exchange Council, and the Mountain States Legal Foundation. Most legal scholars say the bill has the legal weight of helium, but we live in strange times. One thing we have learned in recent years is that a lie, repeated often enough, becomes the truth for those who don't bother to ask too many questions. We also have a Supreme Court that leans far to the right.

Not all battles for access take place in the open. Because some stream access laws are local, a disgruntled land owner can deny entry with a stroke of a pen, a cheap padlock, a few well-placed signs. A county road leads to good water with shady pools and some nice fish. Over time, the road falls into disrepair and dour landowners put up fences and signs, until the road itself begins to look like a private drive that leads to nowhere. Maybe only a handful of locals have fished there, and as they die off or move away, the place passes from memory.

In Wyoming, state legislators have created a safe haven for billionaires and oligarchs who have begun to snap up mountain homes and create "conservation zones" on adjacent property, giving them a tax break and a personal forest out their back door. Others shut gates and let their attorneys deal with the fallout. And then there is the trigger-happy rancher.

"I would never say you're going to get shot, but you could get shot *at*," said Rob Parkins, of Backcountry Hunters & Anglers. "It gets Western."

The trigger-happy rancher might not recognize federal law. He might not recognize the authority of rangers or game wardens who work for the federal government. He only answers to the local sheriff, who happens to be a good friend. These constables call themselves "Constitutional Sheriffs," though the Constitution says nothing about them. They may not have the law on their side, but then again, they might, because laws governing stream access often traverse dark and winding roads.

This is complicated. Public lands fall under federal jurisdiction, but stream access varies from state to state. History has painted Western maps in many colors, a checkerboard that reflects the days of government largess and various title holders that emerged over time: tribal, private, federal, and so on. Underneath this grid is a hodgepodge of regulation based on state and federal statutes, county code, high water marks, case law, policy, politics, the bureaucratic mire.

A court case can change the legal framework of a given state overnight, which means the legislature must interpret the court ruling, Parkins said, which may or may not bring clarity. It's easy to lose focus, given the complexity of these issues, but most battles over access share a common thread:

"It always comes down to money."

Climate change and access could radically alter angling and other forms of outdoor recreation in the West, not in some distant future, but in a decade or two. Vigilance will remain necessary in this new world, a network of local advocacy groups backed by state and national organizations with legal war chests: Trout Unlimited, Backcountry Hunters & Anglers, the Public Land Water Access Association, the Theodore Roosevelt Conservation Partnership, the Center for Western Priorities, to name a few. But anglers, too, are bad at organizing, and the undertow of apathy is strong.

We will also need to behave ourselves because something else plays out in these stories that we don't talk about much. Some people who close gates are old folks who worked like the devil, bought themselves a nice place in the woods, and have grown sick of hooligans overrunning their property.

Some bad actors show up in the hordes that visit our national forests each weekend. Something about the Great Wide Open brings out the worst in these people. They want to ride the range and imagine it is all theirs; they want to pass a bottle of whiskey in the night and howl; they want to believe they are strong, with the gods on their side; they want to rail against the state, shoot pistols in the air, hear bones and pottery chips break under the wheels, poach a deer, take the backstraps, and leave the carcass to rot. The grass is tinder dry, and the feds have banned open flames until the rains come. No matter. These weekend warriors will drink beer around a raging bonfire. On Sunday, they must go back to their real lives, so they pack their gear and drive away, leaving the empties and beds of red-hot coals behind.

They are out there, "and they ruin it for everybody," Parkins said. You can imagine, given how some people behave on public lands, that a few tourists may have strayed onto private property and left trash, failed to close a gate, started a wildfire, shot a cow, parked the boat, lunched in someone's backyard, pissed in front of the kids and the missus. Some anglers, emboldened by their knowledge of civil law, abandon civil behavior and common courtesy. They go fishing, and when a rancher comes by, they do not say hello or wave. They flip him the bird. We can't have it both ways. If we want access we should behave ourselves and not leave a mess.

"How can we," Miles Nolte writes, "as sportsmen who rely on public land and water, expect to maintain our access if the broader community of landowners perceives us as threatening and oppositional?"

> We have woven ourselves a thick narrative blanket: We assume to represent the will and rights of the majority against a small minority of greedy landowners, and we have spent years congratulating ourselves under the comfort of that blanket. We . . . glorify our perspective and demonize those who disagree with us, but I'm afraid that outside our insulated circles, we are losing ground.

Comes now the landowner, who has formed his own coalition, the Western Landowners Alliance. The group points out that private lands can bring value to wildlife conservation and that recreation can be awful hard on ecosystems. They're right about that last part—lots of places on public lands get loved to death. Some landowners have done conservation work on their property, which could be taken into account before we start drawing lines in the sand and reclaiming water for the masses.

Yet Parkins said that blocking access will not necessarily keep out the bad actors who are already breaking laws.

"You can't legislate stupidity. You're not going to get rid of that," he said. Sometimes that trash left by weekend warriors pushes landowners over the edge. Maybe we can work with these folks before things get ugly, pick up some empties, listen to their story. We really should get to know each other before we start running up legal tabs.

The West keeps getting smaller. Oh sure, it looks the same size on paper, but roads compress distance and barbed wire creates a grid where none existed before, a patchwork of ideas and aspirations. Development has carved up ecosystems, the wide-open spaces tamed and diminished. Climate change, sprawl, demographics and foul political winds have thrown everything up for grabs once again. Anglers pour over the mountains as settlers once did, and they thrash the same tired water while lords barricade themselves in their castles. The smell of money is thick, and America's best idea has become caught up in its worst tendencies, its dark heart, feudal law. Hard to say if the days to come will bring out our best, or our worst, or if the two will be tangled in a mess that someday we'll call history.

You can still find plenty of lakes and streams out there, millions of acres of public land, and all this talk of war chests and case law is exhausting. We all want the same thing—to be there sitting by the fire when night comes to the mountain, looking back on the day as it tails off into memory, the dogs curled up, the glasses poured. We can hear the sound of water, or maybe there is no sound at all, just time passing through the valley. This is as good as it gets, the common ground that will either bring us together or tear us apart.

25. The Wasteland

JUST ONCE I'D LIKE to get a little peace and quiet out here. I've spent hours wrangling big rainbows, and I could use some rest. An autumn storm has whipsawed through the canyon, the weather changing by the hour: rain, sleet, sunny and warm, the chill at dusk, and I've walked a few miles, braced against the current, my mind in tune with nature and all its purple majesty. When my head hits the pillow, I hear the music of a natural gas rig somewhere in the dark, a thrumming that drones on through the night.

The San Juan River looks pretty good from the ground. Mule deer move in and out of willow thickets, herons feed in the shallows, canyon walls glow when the iron-flecked stone turns that warm iconic red that makes Southwestern sunsets so special. In the fall, the cottonwoods turn golden. It's beautiful that time of year.

But the surrounding countryside, never all that scenic to begin with, stands worn and windswept, blue, and gritty. The hilltops have taken a beating and arroyos cut deep. Cattle browse the high desert scrub, the highway rolls out in a sweep of body shops, tire shops, fast food chains, and gas stations. A few liquor stores offer something to dull the senses, and you could sure use a drink after that drive.

Yes, you'll find some of the best trout fishing in the world down the road, but everywhere else it's drill, baby, drill. From the air, the place looks like a war zone. I spotted it once on a flight that passed over New Mexico. You might think that I would recall the meandering river, the braided channels, the cottonwoods, the sprawling shores of Navajo Lake. But the hilltops grabbed my attention that day because the oil and gas industry has seized the countryside and staked so many claims that every hilltop has a rig. Every. Single. Hilltop.

You can't complain too much, or too loudly, about this stuff without crashing into reality. Our society craves water, energy, and crops, so the government squeezes a lot from its vast western holdings. Oil and gas provide jobs in a state that needs all the jobs it can get. We use oil in our trucks, which we need to get to the river, and in the planes that fly us all over creation. Natural gas helps fuel the electrical grid and probably will for years.

Although the Skyview look at the San Juan was a real buzzkill, I continue to fish there. Angling literature refers to all kinds of fishing in the wasteland. The flotsam of urban rivers, canals, and lagoons. Fishing for chubs and eels. Luke Jennings pushes through an iron gate for a night of pike fishing on a lonesome backwater, past the railroad maintenance yard, through another gate, past razor wire and shadow, the soft voices of prostitutes in the gloom, a couple of figures bent over a flickering lighter. In *Fishing Through the Apocalypse*, Matthew L. Miller seeks gar and sturgeon, as well as native trout. His prose keens from dystopian tales and industrial angling to the hope for a brighter future.

We embrace the wasteland in all its forms because our needs are simple: a few fish in the water, healthy, burly, spoiling for a fight. We tolerate the trappings of industry, the highway noise, and the trash in our streams for the same reasons we tolerate it in daily life. It's everywhere, and there's not much you can do about it. So we shut up and fish, crack jokes about fishing a river with old tires and shopping carts, the rumors about condoms at the bottom of a pond you fished as a kid. But it's getting harder to laugh. Maybe it's not funny anymore.

More than a century ago, hunters and anglers saw the consequences of their actions—the overfished waters, the decimated flocks and herds, the future bleak. As other conservation causes searched for an identity, hunters and anglers followed their passions and took charge. They created bag limits and seasons, empowered game wardens to enforce the law. To this day, they open their wallets for licenses, permits, and tags without hesitation.

But conservation has changed in the last few decades. Climate change has cast a shadow over everything, and the house that conservationists built has begun to sag and lean in places. Hunters and anglers don't always agree on what they want. The idea of wilderness, once popular, bipartisan, and simple, has fallen out of fashion. The Endangered Species Act, also popular and bipartisan when it passed, can be a bit of a lightning rod. Hunting and fishing groups remain active in the political arena, yet they must take their place among dozens of constituencies. Conservationists have grown into a fragmented bunch, fiercely independent, easily distracted, suspicious, set in their ways.

But poll after poll shows that Americans support public lands, parks, and wildlife. The outdoor industry has become a *trillion*-dollar enterprise. Together, we are a force on the political landscape. Together, we clean up rivers, tear down dams, bring species back from the brink. But we don't get together all that often, and we don't get nearly as much done when we keep to ourselves.

In Arizona, anglers concerned about the state of angling at Lees Ferry sit at the table with municipal water managers, tribal nations, river rafters, state water departments, and conservation groups dedicated to saving what's left of native fish in the Colorado River. The Bureau of Reclamation, the lead agency at these talks, must balance the needs of all these factions, as well as utilities and big agriculture. Anglers don't have a lot of say here. I once heard someone in a fly shop describe our standing like this: Picture a train rolling down the tracks, full of all the movers and shakers, negotiating for their share of water. Where do anglers fit in? Here they come, furiously pumping a handcar, miles behind the train.

You could say the same about the agencies that manage public lands, the Bureau of Land Management (BLM), and the US Forest Service, which operate under the concept of multiple use. The feds allow a lot of things to happen in the great wide open: hunting, camping, hiking, drilling, logging, mining, grazing. And fishing: Here comes the handcar, rolling down the tracks. Conservationists say that although the multiple-use concept sounds nice in principle, in reality, the agencies place a higher value on mining, drilling, grazing, and logging, which means that recreation in all its forms frequently gets the short end of the stick. The BLM recently adopted a policy that puts conservation on equal footing with industry, which could theoretically mean more opportunities for recreation. Time will tell how it plays out in real life.

Mining entrenched itself as a preeminent use of public lands when Congress passed a vacuous yet succinct mining law in 1872. About that time, cattle producers seized grazing rights and have held them ever since, even after they overstocked the range so badly that cattle died where they stood. Attempts to regulate the industry have fallen short.

Back then, the Department of Interior and the Forest Service had a lot of ground to look after, but there was room for everyone. The landscape began to shrink when automobiles gave Americans the ability to cruise all over the countryside. Oil rigs sprang up on public lands to help keep these tourists moving. The agencies juggled all of the uses and user-groups enthusiastically, welcoming all-comers with open arms. After the Second World War, however, the economy boomed, the population rose, and people started to move west. Loggers clamored to harvest more trees grown on federal lands. The newcomers got out to hunt and fish and ramble around the countryside, and sometimes bumped up against abandoned mines and clear cuts, overgrazed ground, and so on. Then the public rallied to the cause of conservation in all its forms. Some folks began to point out the obvious: As much as we might pine for the old days of small government and endless frontier, we're a big country now, all grown up, and we need to establish a few ground rules for the public domain.

So Congress passed the National Environmental Policy Act, The Wilderness Act, the Refuge Recreation Act, the Federal Land Policy and Management Act, the Multiple-Use Sustained Yield Act, the Public Range Improvement Act of 1978, and the Endangered Species Act. The legislation helped regulate private enterprise on public lands, preserve ground, and protect wildlife and natural resources. It empowered federal agencies to carry out these laws.

Time passed, and industry began to grouse about the new rules. Anyone who has filled out a tax return can sympathize—the feds have a way of creating a swamp where none existed: paperwork, questions, jargon, fees, dense thickets of legal blather, endless delays, death by a thousand papercuts. One must wait for an in-depth environmental study to operate a mine, for example, an inventory of birds, plants, bugs, animals. And water sources, which the mine will more than likely spoil. Contrary to popular belief, government is not supposed to move quickly. It's supposed to deliberate before it acts, but it does eventually take action. In the end, the BLM and the Forest Service, guardians of the public domain, bow to the mining law of 1872, issue the permits, and the digging starts. During the Clinton administration, the feds asked herdsmen to do environmental studies before renewing grazing permits, but Congress quickly neutered these regulations by keeping budgets tight and staffing levels low. When the backlog of paperwork became more than the agency could bear, lawmakers granted an exemption to this rule. Oil and gas outfits need to fill out forms and post bonds, but permits remain so cheap that companies frequently take out leases with no oil or gas underground to inflate their lease portfolios and impress shareholders.

These industries continue to operate on public lands for little or no cost, as they always have. Their chief complaint seems to be that they don't like paperwork. So industry says that it suffers terribly at the hands of the federal government, then drops bags of money into the war chests of various congressmen who then howl about the unfairness of the laws they passed. Rather than change the laws, which might draw attention, Congress cuts funding for agencies that manage public lands.

Congress also frequently introduces bills to water down or repeal the ESA. These proposals die on the vine because most lawmakers understand that the American people support the act, and overturning it could backfire. Rather than repeal the ESA, Congress starves the US Fish and Wildlife Service, one of the agencies responsible for carrying out the act, but few people notice. Congress has starved the BLM for decades with little opposition. Lawmakers lowball spending on wildlife refuges, which remain popular with the American public, and the silence is deafening. Lawmakers count on this.

These issues are complex and difficult to follow. Most Americans are too busy to keep track of agency budgets or behind-the-scenes rulemaking or policy changes or the day-to-day operations of federal land agencies. News reports rarely do justice to the various lawsuits filed over public lands. We tend to lose sight of the big picture, and pretty soon it all blurs together. But a lot of waste and malfeasance goes on out there, and it affects watersheds, fish, and wildlife populations profoundly.

Although natural gas production leaks methane, a major driver of climate change, the leaks continue simply because it's cheaper to burn the methane or release it than fix the leak. We have cattle grazing in the desert, which has little or no grass and gets about seven inches of rain a year. Yes, we all need to eat, but these cows contribute virtually nothing to the nation's food supply, though they add significantly to methane levels. We have a long legacy list of cleanups, paid for by the American taxpayer, past, present and future: abandoned gas wells, abandoned uranium and copper mines, toxic waste.

The various boondoggles point to a broken system, but they do not tell the whole story. Occasionally you read about a mining conglomerate that takes on a legacy mine reclamation project, cleaning up a mess it did not make. Or you read about a rancher who does a good job of managing his ground, another who gets on board with a conservation project. Oil and gas companies pay royalties, which get funneled into conservation projects, and big oil reportedly does a good job capping its leaks.

We do need the copper, the oil, the gas. People also need to hike and fish and hunt and ramble around. That's why many of us move west and why wildlife protection and public lands conservation do so well in those polls. The question isn't *should* we dig or drill, or graze or dam or log, but where? Who makes the rules? What does multiple-use really mean?

In 2024, the Colorado College State of the Rockies Project found that 85 percent of Westerners expressed concern about the loss of natural areas. It found that a large majority of Western voters—70 percent—would prefer that Congress emphasize conservation over energy development on public lands. In 2022, the Center for Western Priorities commissioned a poll and found that 90 percent of Westerners care about public lands, parks, and wildlife issues.

Why don't these numbers carry more weight in the political arena? As I have said, conservationists have grown into a fragmented bunch. Ted Williams once wrote about this fragmentation. You can see it in the buzzwords that have crept into our vocabulary, the hallmarks of lazy and distracted thinking: liberal, conservative, tree hugger. Greens, right wingers, socialists, wild-eyed environmentalists, the "antis," who want to take away our guns. Are you an environmentalist or do you work for a living?

We assume that reaching out to this group or that is pointless because they're not like us. We assume that Sierra Club folks won't work with hunters. Williams digs deeper and finds that when you peel back some of these assumptions, you find that nothing is there. The Sierra Club actually welcomes hunters and anglers. So does Audubon.

One problem, Williams writes, is that a bottom-feeding

segment of the hook-and-bullet press fuels these assumptions, and so they continue. Special interests bank on this. Not much has changed since Williams wrote the piece a couple of decades ago, but if it ever does, conservation could be a political force on par with gravity, hurricane winds, or nuclear fusion.

Occasionally we get a glimpse of what is possible. The Cooperative Alliance for Refuge Enhancement has lassoed about two dozen organizations that span the political spectrum, among them the American Birding Association and Ducks Unlimited, Audubon and the National Rifle Association, Trout Unlimited. These groups represent a broad range of interests but have banded together to secure more funding from Congress for the National Wildlife Refuge System. The system remains underfunded, but it gets hundreds of millions of dollars more than it did when CARE formed a few decades ago.

"It can be difficult," said Desirée Sorenson-Groves, President and CEO of the National Wildlife Refuge Association. One reason it's difficult to repeat CARE's formula for success, she said, is that a lot of people don't want consensus, they want conflict. Conflict lends itself to quick and easy sound bites, and funding follows. You can see the same tendency in political ads. People say they hate them, but the ads work, so politicians trot them out every election cycle.

Sorenson-Groves said that CARE's accomplishments prove that people "can work together, but it just takes a lot of work." Then again, she said, just about anything worth doing takes work.

I've asked folks in nongovernment organizations about this many times over the years. Why on earth don't conservation groups put up a more united front? The answer is always a mumble, a shrug, a noncommittal response. Nobody knows.

So I shut up and fish. Yes, there's a shopping cart in the river, an old tire downstream from where that smallmouth took my fly, but what can one person do? A rig sits on every hilltop, but I've gotten a few looks in that seam of feeding fish. They look hungry and burly, spoiling for a fight.

The day will unfold as days on the water usually do. Perhaps the fish will bite, perhaps not, but you can enjoy the changing light, the sunset, the sound of mallards squabbling in a backwater, watch a heron fly off, circle and land across the river. You can still find these moments out there, and you might talk about them in days to come, share them with a loved one or a stranger who will smile and tell you about his last trip to Alaska or her trip to the Rockies. We all have this common language, with different dialects and accents, but the same root words: mountain, stream, fish, birds, elk. We really should get together more.

26. Last Cast

GOOD LORD, HOW QUICKLY the time has passed. It's getting late, and I have squandered another day on the water. The sun has gone down, the fishing has slowed. Time for a beer. One last cast, to try for that one last fish—the one you'll think about on the drive home. The last cast is a plea to whatever piscatorial gods might be out there. It's a promise, a prayer, a running joke, a big lie, because one last cast follows another until night comes to the high country, and we stand at the water's edge, a little numb, sunburned, cold feet, wondering where the time has gone and why the fish have stopped biting.

Fly-fishing looks like a distraction, but it is actually a way of focusing, a meditation on the water. People call it many things—a way of life, a calling—something we can never put into words, though many have tried.

The "great lure of fly fishing is that it is more of a journey than a quest, a journey with unlimited beginnings and no definite end," Harry Middleton writes.

> The angler hopes for nothing and prays for everything; he expects nothing and accepts all that comes his way. And although he knows all along that he will never sink his hook into a trout stream's true mystery, the desire to try, to cast once more and once more again, is never quenched, for there

> is always that chance that one more cast will carry him beyond skill and luck and bring him untarnished magic.

One last cast, and make it count. Is it untarnished magic we seek? A stream's true mystery? A trout the size of a pot roast? Perhaps it is all of these, or none. We're not really sure.

For me, the journey began decades ago. I didn't have much then, just a gun dog, a beat-up truck, a few books, a little music, an entry-level fly rod with a cheap reel. Until then I had been a bait soaker, a worm fisher, young, curious, eager to learn new things, and set out to catch a good number of fish on this new rig to see whether I actually liked fly-fishing before sinking more of my hard-earned money into it. The reel died when a fish made a deep run and stripped its gears. My heart pounded and the fish sprayed water when I brought her aboard to remove the hook. I already knew that this was more than a hobby.

Over time I acquired a new rod and reel, and a backup, just in case, then a backup to the backup. I added short rods for stream fishing, a stout rod for bass fishing and the occasional saltwater romp. I bought fly boxes, flies, boots, and waders. My shelves filled with books of the how-to-fish variety, the where to, and why. I bought a float tube and sinking line to fish high-country lakes, won a kick boat in a raffle.

One of these days I will buy a vessel for big water and bigger fish, perhaps a drift boat, which I'll call the Rusty Spinner, a set of oars and a backup, anchor, life jackets, trailer, a long-handled carbon-fiber net for big fish. Or maybe I'll buy an aluminum beater and call her the Rusty Kettle, with fresh rivets and a sturdy outboard, trolling motor and battery, spare gas can, a set of flares. Sweet Baby Jesus, I can see it now, nothing but clear skies, the wind at my back, broad-shouldered trout rolling in the foam.

I must learn to cut through the clutter—in my closet and in my life. I must up my game, learn to be stealthier, sight fish for hogs, focus, and stop wasting time. Or maybe I will nap by the stream, watch raptors wheel above, and listen to the water—think about the world out there, how things look so peaceful while everything is in motion: plants, bugs, birds, fish. Summer passes and the weather changes, the hills stripped bare, cold that goes to the bone, sluggish trout.

Every autumn I set out in a truck loaded with food and drink, rods and reels, boots, backpack, sleeping bag, maps, books, paper, pens, camera, tripod, the dogs curled up in their kennels, shotgun and shells, the gas tank full, pedal to the metal. Onward! North, by God, north by northeast, where the air is cool and thin, where the roads lead to nowhere and storm clouds gather on yonder mountain.

We drive, and the talk ranges over various topics but, sooner or later, gets around to fishing, perhaps the weather, not small talk but the brass tacks of comfort and survival, such as whether it's a good idea to make camp in a northern squall when the forecast looks so grim.

So we pull over to have a bite and think it through, step into a room abuzz with talk, the clatter of plates and forks, the smell of coffee and bacon, chairs scraping the floor, the table damp where someone has wiped it when out of nowhere a woman's voice says, "What can I getcha, Hon?" We order eggs over easy, bacon, hash browns, something that will stick to the ribs, as they say, while the talk continues.

Maybe we should get a room. There's a reluctance to do this because we have spent all our money on gear and alcohol. This is why so many fly-fishers live like dirtbags when they travel—sleeping under the stars. Home is where they hang their leaky waders, a moving base camp of old trucks and tarps. The scent of wet dog and woodsmoke hangs in the damp air alongside hopes and dreams.

The weather clears, we stick to the plan, drive until we run out of pavement, drive some more. The road, such as it is, rolls out in ruts and rocks, with a few axle benders, but it leads to good water, to where the fish bite like crazy.

We learn to walk this fine line between luck and skill and how the two might mesh. That remains part of the mystery, the joy, the magic, which seems timeless, though times change.

Somewhere along the way I began to look around and notice changes on the horizon. Drought, climate change, mass extinction, sprawl, falling reservoirs. It became hard to ignore the fact that our little outdoor adventures do not take place on pristine waters, that the West is shrinking. The things we love have come under a great deal of stress, sometimes threatening our love for the outdoors, sometimes because of it. A new wave of grifters has swapped history for folk tales and moved in to seize the public domain.

"We have reached a time in the life of the planet, and humanity's demands upon it, when every fisherman will have to be a riverkeeper, a steward of the marine shallows, a watchman on the high seas. . . . We must put back more than we take out," McGuane notes in *The Longest Silence*. The book was published in 1999, and our appetites have only grown. Things once on the horizon now show up in the rearview; the future has arrived. The temperature rises, the forests burn, the stream banks look tired and trampled. Some researchers believe we have entered the Anthropocene, the age of man; others say we have entered the Homogenocene, the age of gray birds, weeds, and diminished wildlife populations; still others the Sixth Extinction, a human-caused genocide of life on the planet. None of these researchers deny that the situation looks bleak—they just can't agree on how bleak, on what to call this mess. It's getting harder to look away.

I'm grateful for all that fly-fishing has given me. I hope that it survives into the next millennium, not as a sport for those who can afford to fish private water but for anyone willing to jump in the truck and go. I've got a few miles left in these legs, a truck that runs. Someday I will buy a skiff that I will call the Rusty Bucket, load her up with tackle and supplies, set a course for a distant cove.

I promised that the dog doesn't die at the end. Chances, though, are fair that by the time this thin tome gets published and it's in your hands, he will no longer be with us. For the moment, he's curled up in the next room as I write, his best days behind him. Let us imagine him in his prime, chasing fly lines at the river's edge. Or we're walking up a hill. There's good brown trout water below us, and he goes on point. When I step forward a covey of Montezuma quail scatters. I have no gun, just a fly rod. We watch them fly away. Good dog.

These memories. But nothing lasts in this world. Even when Pangea linked continents, birds, mammals, and fish made their way, the chain of life never stopped. Who can say when the gods made the first trout? *Eosalmo driftwoodensis,* the ancestor, destroyer of respectable lives. Whenever it was, we should be grateful. One last cast. Everything has led us to this stream, where time has no meaning and days pass through still water.

Acknowledgments

Fly-fishing looks like a solitary pursuit, but even the self-taught angler sorts through gear, flies, and techniques that have been passed down over centuries of angling tradition. The writer who pounds away at the keyboard also appears to work alone, but the truth is that most of us follow trails that others blaze, then consult with editors who help clean up the mess we've made. Most of us could use a little help. God knows I did. So here is a list of people I would like to thank.

Ron Robinson and Steve Stevens of the Arizona Flycasters. Ron and Steve have gone on to the great tailwater in the sky, but they taught me and countless others a lot about fly-fishing over the years. John Rohmer, who walked me through a number of fly-fishing stories. Cinda Howard, who also helped me with stories and read a draft of this manuscript. Matt Swan, Brad Shallenberger, and Emerson Craig, who were kind enough to help let me tag along on a few trips over the years. Fly shop dudes, biologists, NGO folks everywhere.

Jason Benedict, who was always willing to strap on a pack, string up a fly rod, and go see what was out there. It was Jason who said that Luke was the worst fishing dog ever, though I don't think Luke heard and would not have taken offense if he had.

The late Chris Smith, my history professor at Arizona State University, who taught me not to take fishing too seriously. Russ Lumpkin and James Babb, who worked on early versions of some of these stories when they were at *Gray's Sporting Journal*. Various editors and colleagues at *The Arizona Republic* who sent me out on the road and helped shape the stories I came back with. Chad Snow, Al Macias, and my colleagues at KJZZ, the Phoenix NPR affiliate, who picked me up off the street and launched my brief radio career. Stephen Hull and Brenton Woodward of the University of New Mexico Press, who plucked this manuscript out of a firehose of submissions, gave me an opportunity, and helped shape this work; James Cruise was my editor. And Jill Cassidy, who frequently put up with my nonsense along the way and was always happy to tell me, over drinks, when I was wrong.

Headwaters

First Cast

I've got to get out of here: Suzanne K. Fish and Paul R. Fish, eds., *The Hohokam Millennium* (School for Advanced Research Press, 2007), 1–4.

As it turns out: Edward O. Wilson. *Biophilia* (Harvard University Press, 1984), 101; Roger S. Ulrich, "View Through a Window May Influence Recovery from Surgery," *Science* 224 (April 1984): 420–21; Ruth Ann Atchley, David L. Strayer, Paul Atchley, "Creativity in the Wild: Improving Creative Reasoning through Immersion in Natural Settings," *PLoS ONE* 7 (December 2012): 1–3.

Historians: Paul Schullery, *American Fly Fishing: A History* (Lyons and Burford, The American Museum of Fly Fishing, 1987), 7.

People describe: To read about the appeal of fly-fishing, see Paul Schullery, *Royal Coachman: The Lore and Legends of Fly-fishing* (Simon and Schuster, 1999), 1; David Coggins, *The Optimist: A Case for the Fly Fishing Life* (Scribner, 2021), 2–12; John Gierach, *Trout Bum* (Simon and Schuster, 1986), 2–13; Mark Kurlansky, *The Unreasonable Virtue of Fly Fishing* (Bloomsbury, 2021), 18–19. For an academic perspective, see Jen Corrine Brown, *Trout Culture* (University of Washington Press, 2015).

Ted Leeson: Ted Leeson, ed., *The Gift of Trout* (Lyons and Burford, 1996), vii-viii.

Old Trucks, Leaky Waders, Duct Tape

Maybe I'm overthinking: Izaak Walton and Charles Cotton, *The Compleat Angler, or, The Contemplative Man's Recreation* (1653) (Modern Library, 1998), 24.

Is fly-fishing: Schullery, *Royal Coachman*, 129.

"Fly-Fishing is: Schullery, *Royal Coachman*, 1.

Maybe we: Walton, *Compleat Angler*, 25.

Clutter

Journalists and academics: Eva M. Selhub and Alan C. Logan, *Your Brain on Nature: The Science of Nature's Influence on Your Health, Happiness, and Vitality* (John Wiley, 2012); Johann Hari, *Stolen Focus: Why You Can't Pay Attention—and How to Think Deeply Again* (Crown, 2022); Franklin Foer, *World Without Mind: The Existential Threat of Big Tech* (Penguin, 2017).

Hard Work, Dumb Luck, Little White Lies

Some anglers: Veronica Gomez and Lawrence Goldstone, *Lefty: An American Odyssey* (Ballantine, 2012), xix.

"One of the things: John Gierach, *No Shortage of Good Days* (Simon & Schuster, 2011), 6.

A lot of people: Gomez and Goldstone, *Lefty*, xvii, 3–4, 12.

Our obsession: Thomas McGuane, *The Longest Silence* (Vintage, 1999), ix.

"What happens: McGuane, *Longest Silence*, xii.

Sloth

The same: Henry David Thoreau, *Walden, or, Life in the Woods, and On the Duty of Civil Disobedience* (repr., New American Library, 1960), 97.

The slothful angler: Thoreau, *Walden*, 79; McGuane, *Longest Silence*, 121.

I've seen: "An Influencer Rows Through It," *Angling Trade*, April 6, 2021.

An arrogance: Kirk Wallace Johnson, *The Feather Thief: Beauty, Obsession and the Natural History Heist of the Century* (Penguin, 2018), 59–60.

Stealth

In Fly Fishing Small Streams: John Gierach, *Fly Fishing Small Streams* (Stackpole Books, 1989), 33–51.

"I do not: Gierach, *Small Streams*, 44.

"Current is: McGuane, *Longest Silence*, 89–99.

In Fishing Bamboo: John Gierach, *Fishing Bamboo: One Man's Love Affair with Bamboo Fly Rods* (Lyons Press, 1997), 70.

Patience can amount: Tom Rosenbauer, *Fly Fishing for Trout: The Next Level* (Stackpole Books, 2017), 61–64.

It Beats Working

"At its core: Kirk Deeter, "Is Fly-Fishing an 'Elitist' Pursuit?" *Trout*, January 11, 2023.

Trout Chowder

Fly-fishers: Walton, *Compleat Angler*, 57–63.

Another discussion: Paul Schullery, *If Fish Could Scream* (Stackpole Books, 2008), 125–33.

Some of us: Schullery, *If Fish*, 165.

Animal rights: Malachy Tallack, *Illuminated by Water: Fly Fishing and the Allure of the Natural World* (Pegasus Books, 2022), 171–74.

Our obsession: Willa Cather, *Death Comes for the Archbishop* (Vintage, 1971), 38–39.

A few years ago: Ron Carlson, *The Hotel Eden: Stories* (W. W. Norton, 1997), 180–81.

Fishing began: Roderick L. Haig-Brown, *A River Never Sleeps* (Skyhorse Publishing, 2010), 274.

The Backcountry

The academic: Sherry Simpson, *The Accidental Explorer: Wayfinding in Alaska* (Sasquatch Books, 2008), 10–11.

All the Fish We Cannot See

(With apologies to Anthony Doerr)

In The Old Man and the Sea: Ernest Hemingway, *The Old Man and the Sea* (Charles Scribner's Sons, 1952), 74–89.

"He can't be: Hemingway, *Old Man*, 89–90, 97.

Several times: Hemingway, *Old Man*, 66, 75, 95.

That is the deal: Kirk Deeter, "Is Catch-and-Release Angling All It's Cracked Up to Be?" *Trout*, May 28, 2021.

Fishing is a con: Ed Engle, *Fly Fishing the Tailwaters* (Stackpole Books, 1991).

Autumn Splendor

The Western economy: "Commerce's Bureau of Economic Analysis Reports Outdoor Recreation Economy Tops $1 Trillion in 2022," US Department of Commerce, December 15, 2023, News Release.

"Fall gives us a vague feeling that: McGuane, *Longest Silence*, 97.

Rock 'n' Roll Hill

Some of my: Tim Wu, "The Tyranny of Convenience," *New York Times*, February 16, 2018, Sunday Review.

James Babb: James R. Babb, *Fish Won't Let Me Sleep* (Skyhorse Publishing, 2016), 128–33; Brown, *Trout Culture*, 75–77.

Animals

"Fishing is a quest: Paul Schullery, *The Fishing Life: An Angler's Tales of Wild Rivers and Other Restless Metaphors* (Skyhorse Publishing, 2013), 28.

Research confirms: See Stephen R. Kellert and Edward O. Wilson, eds., *The Biophilia Hypothesis* (Island Press, 1993); Selhub and Logan, *Your Brain*; Roger S. Ulrich, "View Through a Window May Influence Recovery from Surgery," *Science* 224 (April 1984): 420–21; Ruth Ann Atchley, David L. Strayer, and Paul Atchley, "Creativity in the Wild: Improving Creative Reasoning through Immersion in Natural Settings." *PLoS ONE* 7 (December 2012): 1–3.

Wild Roses

The fire started: "Hell Comes to White Mountains: How 'Rodeo' and 'Chediski' Burned Their Names into Arizona History," *Arizona Republic*, June 30, 2002; Tom Zoellner, *Rim to River: Looking into the Heart of Arizona* (University of Arizona Press, 2023), 136–42.

Somewhere: Zoellner, *Rim to River*, 138–39; "Hiker's Fire is Thorny Legal Issue," *Arizona Republic*, July 11, 2002. Accounts vary on how long Elliott spent in the woods.

Lake Solitude

We really do: "The Forbidding Reputation and Hypnotic Scenery of the Devil's Highway," *New York Times*, April 29, 2019.

Edward Abbey: "Burying Edward Abbey: The Last Act of Defiance," *Arizona Republic*, April 17, 2015.

The other Devil's Highway: "US 666: Revisiting the Devil's Highway," ADOT Communications, Oct. 29, 2023; "U.S. Route 191, White Mountains," *Arizona Highways*, https://www.arizonahighways.com/coronado-trail, accessed December 11, 2024; "Renaming U.S. 666 Prompts a Run on 'Satanic' Souvenirs," *New York Times*, July 20, 2003.

After a while: "Wallow Fire 2011, Large Scale Event Recovery, Rapid Assessment Team, Fire/Report, Apache-Sitgreaves National Forests," US Forest Service, July 29, 2011.

Yellow Trout

Apache trout: *Apache Trout Recovery Plan, Second Revision*, US Fish and Wildlife Service (Albuquerque, 2009), v., 1–6; Robert Rush Miller, "Classification of the Native Trouts of Arizona with the Description of a New Species, Salmo apache," *Copeia* 3 (September 1972): 401–22.

In 1965: Papers of the Presidents, Manuscripts Division, Library of Congress, December 17, 1965; Christmas Pageant of Peace, NPS-WESF, RG 79, BOX 21, A8227, January 1, 1966, Part 1, Letter, January 19, 1966; Christmas Pageant of Peace, NPS-ESF, RG 79, BOX 18, A8227, US Department of Interior, Press Release, October 17, 1965; Christmas Pageant of Peace, NPS-WESF, RG 79, BOX 18, file 1115–27, A8227, Letter, December 14, 1965.

The tribe had: *Apache Trout Recovery Plan*, 1.

The council had: W. L. Minckley and James E. Deacon, eds., *Battle Against Extinction: Native Fish Management in the American West* (University of Arizona Press, 1991), 12.

By this time: *Apache Trout Recovery Plan*, 1; Mitch Tobin, *Endangered: Biodiversity on the Brink* (Fulcrum Publishing, 2010), 43–48.

When Congress passed: Endangered Species Act (ESA), 1973; Tobin, *Endangered*, 43–49; Zygmunt J. B. Plater, "Tiny Fish, Big Battle," *Tennessee Bar Journal* (April 2008): 14–42; Proceedings of the Endangered Species Committee, Archival Materials, Paper 2 United States Department of Interior (1979), 7, Lawdigitalcommons.bc.edu/darter materials/2; Zygmunt J. B. Plater, "Tiny Fish/Big Battle: 30 Years After TVA and the Snail Darter Clashed, the Case Still Echoes in Caselaw, Politics and Popular Culture," *American Currents* 34 (2008): 1–7.

At the time: Marc Reisner, *Cadillac Desert: The American West and Its Disappearing Water* (Penguin, 1993), 324–30.

When nobody: Tobin, *Endangered*, 48–49.

The ESA: Tobin, *Endangered*, 8, 55.

Fish and Wildlife delisted: Federal Register, 89, no. 173, US Department of Interior, Fish and Wildlife Service, 50 CFR Part 17, Final Rule, September 6, 2024.

Gila Trout

The Gila Trout's ancestors: *Gila Trout Recovery Plan*, US Fish and Wildlife Service (New Mexico Ecological Services State Office, Albuquerque, 1993), 2–9; David L. Propst, Jerome A. Stefferud, and Paul R. Turner, "Conservation and Status of Gila Trout, Oncorhynchus gilae," *Southwestern Naturalist* 37 (June 1992): 117–25.

By this time: Anders Halverson, *An Entirely Synthetic Fish: How Rainbow Trout Beguiled America and Overran the World* (Yale University Press, 2011).

Rainbow trout adapt: Halverson, *Synthetic Fish*, 79.

Rainbow trout don't: *Gila Trout Recovery Plan*, 26–27. Western Native Trout Status Report, Arizona Game and Fish Department, New Mexico Game and Fish Department, US Fish and Wildlife Service, US Forest Service, updated 2016.

Fishheads historically assumed: Halverson, *Synthetic Fish*, 117–22.

While biologists: David E. Brown and Neil B. Carmony, eds., *Aldo Leopold's Wilderness* (Stackpole Books, 1991), 143–44; Paul S. Sutter. "'A Blank Spot on the Map': Aldo Leopold, Wilderness, and the U.S. Forest Service Recreational Policy, 1909–1924," *Western Historical Quarterly* 29 (Summer 1998): 189–90; Stephen J. Pyne, *Smokechasing* (University of Arizona Press, 2003), 108; Paul Schullery, "The Fires and Fire Policy," *BioScience* 39 (November 1989).

As fishery biologists: John N. Rinne, "Wildfire in the Southwestern USA: Effects on Fishes," 2nd International Wildland Fire Ecology and Fire Management Congress 2003, 1–5. D. Kendall Brown et. al., "Catastrophic Wildfire and Number of Populations as Factors Influencing Risk of Extinction for Gila Trout (Oncorhynchus gilae)," *Western North American Naturalist* 61, no. 2 (2001): 139–48.

Fire on the Mountain

Researchers say: Bingbing Xu, Jeffrey A. Hicke, and John T. Abatzoglou, "Drought and Moisture Availability and Recent Western Spruce Budworm Outbreaks in the Western United States," *Forests* 10, no. 4 (2019): 354; Cheryl Katz, "Small Pests, Big Problems: The Global Spread of Bark Beetles," *YaleEnvironment360* (September 21, 2017).

Three of America's: J. E. Williams et al., "Cold-Water Fishes and Climate Change in North America," *Reference Module in Earth System and Environmental Sciences* (Elsevier, 2015); Jack E. Williams et al. "State of the Trout," *Trout Unlimited* (2015); Steven Kinsella, Theo Spencer, and Bruce Farling, "Trout in Trouble: The Impacts of Global Warming on Trout in the Interior West," Natural Resources Defense Council, Issue Paper (July 2008).

The Fossil Record: Robert J. Behnke, *Trout and Salmon of North America* (Free Press, 2002), 2–3.

They took the bait: Sutter, "'A Blank Spot,'" 189–90. Brown, "Catastrophic Wildfire," 139–48.

Climate change: Seth J. Wenger et al., "Flow Regime, Temperature, and Biotic Interactions Drive Differential Declines of Trout Species Under Climate Change," *PNAS* 108 (August 2011); "Trout in Trouble," 4–7; Brad Trumbo and Mark Hudy et al., "Sensitivity and Vulnerability of Brook Trout Populations to Climate Change," Wild Trout Symposium, Conserving Wild Trout (2010); S. A. Spaulding and L. Elwell, "Increase in Nuisance Blooms and Geographic Expansion of the Freshwater Diatom *Didymosphenia geminata*," (US Geological Survey Open-File Report 2007), 1425.

Some scientists: Robert H. Cowie, Philippe Bouchet, and Benoit Fontaine, "The Sixth Mass Extinction: Fact, Fiction or Speculation?" *Biological Reviews* 97 (2022).

But anglers: Farling, "Trout In Trouble," 7.

No Trespassing

Public lands: Testimony of Trout Unlimited on the Public Land Renewable Energy Development Act, H.R. 3326. Expanding Clean Energy on Public Lands, US Congress, House Natural Resources Committee on Energy and Mineral Resources Subcommittee hearing, May 24, 2021.

Americans have looked: Stephen E. Ambrose, *Undaunted Courage: Meriwether Lewis, Thomas Jefferson, and the Opening of the American West* (Simon and Schuster, 1997), 51–57.

Congress understood: Digital History, American Land Policy, ID 3836; James Muhn and Hanson R. Stuart, *Opportunity and Challenge: The Story of BLM* (US Department of Interior, 1988), 13–14.

As new territories: John D. Leshy, "Are U.S. Public Lands Unconstitutional?" *Hastings Law Journal* 69 (2018).

The nation: Leshy, 36.

Congress spent: Bernard DeVoto, *DeVoto's West: History, Conservation, and the Public Good* (Swallow Press, 2005), 79.

But the land: Federal Land Policy and Management Act of 1976, Public Law 94-579, 94th Congress.

Sagebrush Rebels: Christopher Ketcham, *This Land: How Cowboys, Capitalism, and Corruption are Ruining the American West* (Viking, 2019), 120–21.

The movement: Jonathan P. Thompson, *Sagebrush Empire: How a Remote Utah County Became the Battlefront of American Public Lands* (Torrey House Press, 2021), 159–65.

But the movement: Utah Legislature, H.J.R. 3, Joint Resolution on Federal Transfer of Public Lands, General Session State of Utah, 2012; "The Larger, but Quieter Than Bundy, Push to Take Over Federal Land," New York Times, January 10, 2016; American Lands Council, Public Policy Statement.

In Wyoming: Justin Farrell, *Billionaire Wilderness: The Ultra-Wealthy and the Remaking of the American West* (Princeton University Press, 2020), 85–88;

""The 'Cowboy Cocktail': How Wyoming Became One of the World's Top Tax Havens," Pandora Papers, December 20, 2021.

"How can we: "Stream Access Now: A report on stream access laws state by state," Backcountry Hunters and Anglers (2017), 12.

Comes now: Western Landowners Alliance, Public Access Policy Statement.

The Wasteland

Although the Skyview: Luke Jennings, *Blood Knots: A Memoir of Fathers, Friendship, and Fishing* (Skyhorse Publishing, 2012), 1–2; Matthew Miller, *Fishing Through the Apocalypse: An Angler's Adventures in the 21st Century* (Lyons Press, 2019); Greg Keeler, *Trash Fish: A Life* (Counterpoint, 2008), 31.

More than a century ago: Philip Shabecoff, *A Fierce Green Fire: The American Environmental Movement* (Hill and Wang, 1993), 74–84; Schullery, American Fly Fishing, 124–28.

But poll: "Commerce's Bureau of Economic Analysis Reports Outdoor Recreation Economy Tops $1 Trillion in 2022," US Department of Commerce, December 15, 2023, News Release.

You could say: Federal Register 89, no. 91 (2024), 40308. Department of the Interior. Bureau of Land Management, Conservation and Landscape Health.

Mining entrenched itself: Mining Act of May 10, 1872, rev. statutes of the United States.

Back then: Paul Hirt, *A Conspiracy of Optimism: Management of the National Forests Since World War Two* (University of Nebraska Press, 1994).

So Congress passed: Multiple-Use Sustained Yield Act of 1960, US Congress, Public Law 86–517; Refuge Recreation Act of 1962, US Congress, Public Law 87–714; The Wilderness Act of 1964, US Congress, Public Law 88–570; National Environmental Policy Act of 1969, US Congress, Public Law 91–190; Endangered Species Act of 1973, US Congress, Public Law 93–205; Federal Land Policy and Management Act of 1976, US Congress, Public Law 94–579.

Time passed: "Grazing Fees: Overview and Issues," Congressional Research Service, RS21232. 2019; "Grazing Fees: Overview and Issues," Congressional Research Service, RS21232. 2016; End Speculative Oil and Gas Leasing Act of 2021, S. 607, 117th Congress, First Session.

Congress also frequently: "Endangered Species Act Implementation: Science or Politics?" Committee on Natural Resources, US House of Representatives, One hundred tenth Congress, First Session, May 9, 2007, ser. no. 110–24.

Although natural gas production: "Inflation Reduction Act Methane Emissions Charge: In Brief," Congressional Research Service, R47206. 2022; "Biden Administration to Fine Oil and Gas Companies for Excess Methane," *New York Times*, January 12, 2024; "Methane-Spewing Gas and Oil Drillers Owe the U.S. Billions—in Theory," *Mother Jones*, February 22, 2024; Western Watersheds Project et al. v. United States Bureau of Land Management, 2:21-CV-01126-SRB; "Abandoned Mines: Information on the Number of Hardrock Mines, Cost of Cleanup, and Value of Financial Assurances," US Government Accountability Office, 2011. "Orphaned Wells Program Annual Report to Congress," US Department of Interior, 2024.

In 2024: Colorado College: "State of the Rockies Project," Conservation in the West Poll, 2024; Center for Western Priorities, "Winning the West: Public Attitudes on Public Lands, Recreation and Energy," 2022.

Why don't: "Guns and Greens," *Audubon* (January/February 2005); Richard White, *Uncommon Ground: Rethinking the Human Place in Nature* (W. W. Norton, 1996), 171.

Occasionally we get: Cooperative Alliance for Refuge Enhancement, *A History of CARE*, 2020.

Last Cast

The "great lure: Harry Middleton, *The Earth is Enough: Growing Up in a World of Flyfishing, Trout, and Old Men* (Simon and Schuster, 1989; WestWinds Press, 1996), 79.

"We have reached: McGuane, *Longest Silence*, xii.

These memories: Behnke, *Trout and Salmon*, 1–2.

www.ingramcontent.com/pod-product-compliance
Lightning Source LLC
LaVergne TN
LVHW090946080826
845145LV00003B/903